The

Cookbook

We praise all the flowers that we fancy
Sip the nectar of fruit ere they're peeled,
Ignoring the common old tater
When, in fact, he's King of the Field.
Let us show the old boy we esteem him,
Sort of dig him up out of the mud;
Let us show him he shares our affections
And crown him with glory—King Spud.
-Irish Potato Marketing Company

The Potato Cookbook

Janet Reeves

PELICAN PUBLISHING COMPANY

Gretna 1997

Published by Ragweed Press as *One Potato Two Potato,* 1987
Published by arrangement by
    Pelican Publishing Company, Inc., 1997
Not for sale in Canada.

---

*The word "Pelican" and the depiction of a pelican are trademarks
of Pelican Publishing Company, Inc., and are registered
in the U.S. Patent and Trademark Office.*

Library of Congress Cataloging-in-Publication Data

Reeves, Janet.
    The potato cookbook / Janet Reeves.
        p.   cm.
    Includes index.
    ISBN 1-56554-246-0 (pb : alk. paper)
    1. Cookery (Potatoes) 2. Potatoes. I. Title.
TX803.P8R44 1996
641.6'521—dc20
                                        96-38297
                                              CIP

Illustrations: Brenda Whiteway

Manufactured in the United States of America
Published by Pelican Publishing Company, Inc.
1101 Monroe Street, Gretna, Louisiana 70053

Contents

Introduction

This book is an affectionate chronicle of the potato. It tells the story of the potato from its earliest struggle for survival to the attaining of its rightful crown—the World's Number One Vegetable, King Spud.

This rise in fame follows a four-century crusade rife with ignorance, superstition, and fear. Today the potato is a part of our way of life—the average person in North America is said to eat one hundred pounds of potatoes a year—yet not long ago people would starve rather than eat one.

In the potato we find a versatile food that is both nutritious and economical. It is easy to prepare as a side vegetable or in a variety of taste-tempting dishes. No other vegetable is served as often or combines as well with other foods as the potato.

The Potato Cookbook is a fascinating record of the potato's pilgrimage. This book includes historical and nutritional facts, illustrations, numerous pieces of trivia, and helpful hints, as well as nearly three hundred palate-pleasing recipes dedicated to good food from many kitchens, past and present. The recipes included keep to the basic simplicity and naturalness of our pioneer cooks, yet are adapted for use in today's modern kitchens. You will find new ideas for family meals and festive entertaining, with foods ranging from country classica to international gourmet specialties.

Potatoes form the main ingredient of many dishes, while other recipes, such as the baked products, have been modified to benefit from the inclusion of potatoes. The resulting improvement in texture—while at the same time keeping quality, moistness, and flavor—justifies the little extra work involved in using potatoes.

The tested recipes in this book are presented in imperial measurements and can be easily reduced or expanded. However, a metric conversion table is included. Ingredients are listed in order of use and all instructions are clearly stated . . . assuring that every recipe will produce perfect results every time.

Few foods can rival the versatile potato. After researching and writing this book, I, for one, will never again take the potato for granted. The "lowly spud" is indeed "King."

THE POTATO COOKBOOK

The Potato Cookbook

The History of the Potato

No one knows the exact origin of the potato. Potato researchers and archaeologists believe that some form of potato was cultivated as far back as 500 B.C. We naturally assume the potato has always been with us, yet the first recorded knowledge of potatoes being used as a staple food goes back just over four centuries, to the Spanish invasion of South America. Little did the conquistadores know that when they went looking for gold, they would also find buried treasure in the potato.

The Incas had found the plants growing wild at altitudes too cold for wheat and corn. They cultivated them and developed some nearly frost-proof varieties. Potatoes were an important part of the Inca way of life. They were used for telling time, treatment of illness and injury, divination, fermenting into drinks, and for their main food. The Incas worshipped potato deities. They celebrated rituals and offered occasional human sacrifices to appease the gods. When crops failed, noses and lips of some of the natives were mutilated in ceremonies dedicated to the potato gods. Many early Indian pottery designs also combine potato and human forms.

The Peruvian name for the plant is *papa,* meaning "tuber." The Quechua language has over a thousand words to describe potatoes. For example, a long flat potato is called *mishipasinghan* (cat's nose). Misshapen, hard-to-prepare potatoes are *lumchipamundana* (potatoes make young bride weep).

The Incas used potatoes to prepare what was probably the first freeze-dried food. *Chuño* (choon-yo) is still produced in the highlands of Bolivia, Chile, and Peru, using the same age-old techniques. The Indians take the newly harvested potatoes and spread them on the ground to freeze overnight. The potatoes thaw in the hot morning sun and, at midday, barefoot men, women, and children trample them, squeezing out the excess moisture. The pulp dries in the afternoon sun. This goes on daily for up to three weeks until the potatoes are reduced to a grayish, dry material that resembles small stones. Chuño is as hard as wood, very lightweight, and will keep for up to four years. Grayish chuño *(chuño negro)* is soaked in at least six to eight changes of water to reduce bitterness and then is used in a variety of dishes. White chuño *(chuño tunta* or *moray)* is made by soaking the freeze-dried chuño in streams of running water for several days and then re-drying, removing the gray color.

Today chuño can be bought in crushed, whole, or powdered forms. The powder is used instead of wheat in baking bread. As the Inca saying goes, "stew without chuño is like life without love."

The Incas also sun-dried cooked potatoes to form *papa seca,* an amber-colored granular material that was used in soup stock. These products, with their excellent keeping qualities, were then stored for use by the Inca armies and as insurance against famine.

The Spanish explorers, among them Gonzalo Jemenez de Quesada, found the potato to their liking and after the conquest of Peru brought back both potatoes and Inca gold. The potato received mixed reaction in Spain, including distrust and fear. At first they were grown in Galicia and only as a garden novelty.

Little was known about the potato, giving reason for the people's initial fear. The potato belongs to the botanical family *Solanaceae,* which includes many poisonous narcotic and hallucinogenic relatives such as mandrake and bella donna (also called deadly nightshade). Some potatoes contain solanine, which causes a skin rash that sixteenth-century Europeans thought was the beginning of leprosy. And any food growing underground was thought to be both unclean and unchristian.

Before long, however, the potato began to gain a reputation for some medicinal benefits. Cut potatoes were applied to warts, sprains, and black eyes. In time they were used for rheumatism, scurvy, and as a cure for impotence. Some people, though, still felt potatoes were evil, that they caused flatulence and syphilis, among other things. However, when the potato was labeled as a powerful aphrodisiac, it was on its way—black market prices reached unbelievable heights.

Some of the more adventuresome folk began using potatoes as food around the 1570s. In 1573 potatoes were fed to hospital patients. About this time they were also used for feeding livestock and convicts.

From Spain, the use of the potato spread to Italy, where it was believed that one could dispose of an enemy by writing his name on a potato.

Meanwhile, in 1563, Sir John Hawkins is said to have introduced the potato to England. Its cultivation at this time, however, was sadly neglected. In 1586 the potato was reintroduced, probably by way of one of Sir Francis Drake's ships. England was slow to accept the potato, associating it with squalor. Ironically, it was later thought of as a botanical curiosity and a rich man's delicacy.

In 1619 King James I first served potatoes at the royal table. England introduced potatoes to Flanders during the wars against King Louis XIV. Finally, during the Victorian era, the British upper class bean to take the potato seriously.

King Charles II made efforts, between 1660 and 1685, to have commoners plant potatoes. In 1664 an English author wrote a book to promote the "lowly spud." Entitled (along with several subtitles) *England's Happiness Increased, of a Sure and Easie Remedy Against All succeeding Dear Years by a Plantation of Roots called Potatoes,* the book most likely was *not* a best seller, but it probably has the distinction of having the longest title.

The potato arrived in Germany in 1588. Here it was considered a lowly food, suitable for livestock, prisoners, and common folk. The upper class wanted nothing to do with food associated with the South American Indians that was also grown underground.

In Scotland the clergy found no mention of potatoes in the Bible and banned them because they were "unholy." In Burgundy and Besancon, potatoes were called Indian artichokes and were forbidden, out of fear of leprosy and syphilis.

By the end of the seventeenth century, potatoes had reached Russia, imported from Holland by Peter the Great, and were served at Imperial banquets. The Russian peasants would not eat them and labeled them unclean and unchristian, saying they were "the Devil's apples." A few centuries later, during the Siege of Leningrad, scientists felt potatoes were so important that they burned furniture to keep a sack of precious seed potatoes from freezing. Although near starvation, they refused to eat the small tubers.

In time, the more enlightened people saw the value of the potato and several kings and emperors initiated national programs of potato planting. In 1740 the potato saved the Irish from famine. In 1744 King William of Germany ordered the peasants to plant potatoes. He distributed potatoes free along with instructions on how to plant them. He then sent soldiers to supervise the planting and threatened to cut off the nose of anyone who disobeyed. Twenty years later an official proclamation forced the people of Sweden to grow potatoes. The inhabitants of Kolbery, Germany, however, remained adamant. As late as 1774, they refused to eat the "sexually unclean" potato, despite the fact that they were in a state of famine. Switzerland associated potatoes with scrofula and was also a long time accepting them.

THE POTATO COOKBOOK

A French chemist, Antoine August Parmentier, probably did more than anyone else to promote the potato. Parmentier, a soldier in the French army during the Seven Years' War, was captured and imprisoned in Hanover, Germany, for three years. While in prison, he and his friends lived almost entirely on potatoes—food the Germans fed to livestock. Upon returning to France, Parmentier found his country in a state of famine, yet still unwilling to eat the food that had saved his life. The French thought that potatoes would weaken the people and ruin the land. Parmentier declared this fear nonsense and wrote a thesis to promote the potato. His work, entitled *Inquiry Into Nourishing Vegetables That At Times of Necessity Could Be Substituted for Ordinary Food,* was published in 1773 and listed potatoes among the vegetables that could help in times of food shortages. History reports that Parmentier went to the birthday party of King Louis XVI and presented him with a bouquet of potato blossoms. The king put a flower in his buttonhole and Queen Marie Antoinette wore potato flowers in her hair. Almost immediately the aristocracy copied them and potato flowers became the fashion. Potato designs appeared on pottery, china, and jewelry.

Parmentier then devised a plan to save the country and popularize the potato as a food. He entertained with elaborate banquets, inviting famous people to his home and serving as many as twenty dishes at each meal, all containing potatoes. Next he persuaded the king to give him fifty arpents (about one acre) of barren soil, just outside the city of Les Sablons, near Paris. Parmentier planted potatoes in the sandy soil and, as harvest time approached, stationed guards around the field during the day. At night the guards were taken away. As he expected, the local peasants, curious about something valuable enough to be guarded, began to pilfer the potato patch.

Before long, potatoes were blossoming all over France. Thanks to Parmentier, the potato became one of France's staple foods as well as a status symbol. Parmentier was called the "Potato Messiah," and today the best potato dishes in France have "Parmentier" in their name. After his death, statues were built to honor Parmentier, and for some time potatoes were planted each year on his grave.

By 1813, potatoes were being grown extensively in Scotland and were becoming well-known in Holland, Austria, Switzerland, Germany, and Italy.

Historians disagree on who brought the first potato to Ireland. Some say Sir Francis Drake, others Sir Walter Raleigh, and still others think they were found in shipwrecks of Spanish sailors along the coast. They do agree, however, that they were there by 1663 and were given a generous welcome.

Ireland adopted the reliable, uncomplicated potato more readily than any of her neighbors. Potatoes grow easily and abundantly in cool, moist areas. Ireland's soil and climate are ideal. Here potatoes quickly became a dietary staple and were accepted as a national food. Ireland's population increased steadily and potatoes became such an important food that they were quickly named "Irish" potatoes to distinguish them from sweet potatoes.

The potato also became a secret weapon. During the seventeenth-century rebellions in Ireland, the English soldiers tried to quell uprisings by burning or trampling the food crops. But the potato was safely underground.

In 1740 a crop failure caused a famine that resulted in the deaths of about one-fifth of the population, but it did not force the Irish to give up on potatoes. One hundred years later, the population had risen to an all-time high of about nine million people.

Ironically, the ideal climate for growing potatoes is also the ideal condition for one of the potato's worst enemies. This was to prove devastating to the people of Ireland. Until the 1840s, late blight was unheard of in Ireland. In 1845 tragedy struck all of Europe in a scourge of late blight. Late blight is a fungus that starts in the leaves of the plant. From there, spores go into the soil to attack the tubers, destroying the plant within a week. Late blight, although still a universal problem for potato growers, can be controlled with fungicides. In the 1840s, however, there were no such controls and the worst disaster since the Black Death of 1348 to 1350 occurred. Late blight spread through the country, causing crop failures from 1845 to 1851.

The first two years were the worst as Ireland's crops were a total failure. Unlike the rest of Europe, Ireland depended almost entirely on potatoes for food. They grew grain and raised cattle, but these other products were exported to their absentee landlords in England. Over a million people died of starvation and disease, and hundreds of thousands emigrated to other countries. The actual count of those who died was never determined, as many people also perished at sea. The overcrowded ships came to be known as coffin ships. Today in Ireland you can still see the mounds where people were buried in mass graves.

By the end of the century, steady emigration and fewer births had cut the population of Ireland in half. The majority of the emigrants settled in the United States. Some also came to Canada, along with many English and Scottish settlers, bringing with them the potato.

Others went to Australia; they were the first immigrants in that country who were not convicts.

Potatoes had been brought to North America via Bermuda as early as 1621. There is evidence of potatoes growing in Port Royal, Nova Scotia, as early as 1623. They were not considered an important crop until the Irish immigrants introduced them to New Hampshire in 1719. As late as 1740, North Americans thought potatoes would shorten men's lives.

Immigrants after the "Great Famine" firmly established the potato in North America. Today, in spite of a history telling a distinct lack of enthusiasm, and various famines and disasters, the potato has gained strength. By the end of the nineteenth century, potatoes were considered a superior food. Today they are grown in 130 countries and yield more food on less land than any major crop. They are found almost everywhere in the world, expect for the lowland tropics and the polar ice regions (although they are even found in parts of Greenland). Potatoes are the fourth largest world crop, surpassed only by wheat, rice, and corn.

It is interesting to note that the potato made history in 1979 by being the first produce item to receive a nutrition label. The label gives nutritionists a guide for analyzing other fruits and vegetables. No longer is the potato a "fattening starch" but is recognized as a nutritious, beneficial vegetable that should be included in every well-balanced diet. Children unable to tolerate milk are given potatoes, which provide about 75 percent of their nutritional requirements. Potatoes are being seriously considered as a possible answer to world hunger.

Today the riches of the Inca Empire and the glory of the Spanish conquistadores are only recorded memories. Yet the potato lives on . . . the vegetable that conquered the world.

What Is a Potato?

The potato, *Solanum tuberosum*, is a perennial plant cultivated for its edible starchy tubers. Above the ground the potato has an erect stem with alternately arranged, coarse dark-green compound leaves, resembling those of a tomato. (Tomatoes, along with eggplant, peppers, and tobacco, are part of the same botanical family.) The flowers range in colors of white, pink, red, or bluish-purple, depending on variety. These flowers develop a small green fruit (seed ball), one-half to one inch in diameter, again resembling the tomato's. Each seed ball contains about three hundred yellowish seeds.

Scientists use these seeds, called true potato seed, in developing new varieties of disease-free potato plants. Like its relative, the deadly nightshade, these seed balls and all green parts of the potato plant are poisonous.

Lateral shoots grow from the main stem of the potato down into the ground. Food made in the leaves passes to the end of these shoots, causing them to swell and form tubers. The tuber, or edible part of the potato, is not part of the root as is commonly believed, but is formed by this swelling of the underground stems (or rhizones).

The skin of the potato may range in color from tan and brown to white, red, or purple. The flesh is usually white or light yellowish, with a few varieties having a bluish tinge.

The "eyes" on potatoes are, in fact, tiny leaves and external buds, each of which can produce a new shoot or plant. In North America, potatoes are usually planted by "sets" or "seed pieces" which are portions of potatoes that have at least one to three "eyes" in each piece. These sets are planted in trenches at spaces of 12 to 18 inches, depending on variety. They are covered with a few inches of soil. As the plants grow, additional soil is put up around them to protect the developing tubers. Potatoes require a cool growing season. From the time they are planted it takes from

THE POTATO COOKBOOK

90 to 140 days for potatoes to reach maturity, depending again on variety and location. All seed potatoes should be government-inspected and certified as suitable for planting. The home gardener should not plant potatoes from the supermarket. These potatoes have usually had a sprout inhibitor sprayed on them and thus will not grow. Your local potato grower will be able to provide you with seed potatoes.

Diseases and insect pests that attack potatoes are too numerous to deal with here. Potato beetles, aphids, and blight are just three of the scourges potatoes are susceptible to. However, modern research has developed various chemical and organic sprays and dusts to control most potato-growing problems. Consult your local Department of Agriculture for information on growing potatoes in your area.

Nutritional Value of the Potato

The potato is one of only a few foods capable of nourishing the great populations of the world. Contrary to popular belief, the potato is not fattening. A medium potato cooked with its skin contains only 90 calories (about the same as an apple or pear), yet supplies the following percentage of a recommended daily intake of nutrients:

Vitamin C	=	30%
Iron	=	8 to 10%
Thiamin (B1)	=	10%
Riboflavin (B2)	=	3%
Niacin	=	11%
Protein	=	3%
Calcium	=	3%

Potato carbohydrate and iron is over 90 percent usable. Complex carbohydrates such as those found in the potato are an essential part of a well-balanced diet. The ratio of protein to carbohydrate is higher in potatoes than in many cereals and the protein quality is higher than most other food crops.

A potato has about the same amount of Vitamin C as a glass of tomato juice; its iron content is equivalent to that found in an egg; and it is low in sodium and 99.9 percent fat-free.

Many nutritionists agree that when starch is substituted for sugar, appetite is reduced; therefore potatoes, which also provide vitamins and minerals, are invaluable in reducing diets.

The following chart includes calorie counts of sample—note the low counts of most potato dishes. The measurement used is 3½ oz.

Food	Calories
Mashed potato	65
Boiled potato (peeled)	65
Whole milk	65
Potato (boiled in skin)	76
Potato (baked in skin)	93
Potato salad with dressing	99
Pork and beans	122
Rice pudding with raisins	146
Ice cream	207
Eggs, fried	216
Whiskey	249
Potatoes, French fried	274
Hamburger, regular	286
Boston Cream Pie	302
Chocolate Chiffon Cake	328
Yellow cake, chocolate icing	365
Choice club steak	380
Pecan pie	418
Potato chips	568
Bacon	611

Note: adding 1 tsp. or a pat of butter to potatoes adds 35 calories.

Buying and Storing Potatoes

Potatoes are graded and packaged under strict government regulations governing quality and size. Select potatoes that are firm, smooth, clean, and uniform in shape, and free from wrinkles, cuts, decay, blemishes, or a green skin. Buy the size best suited to your needs.

Store potatoes in a cool, dry, well-ventilated place. The ideal temperature is 45 to 50 degrees. Be sure to store potatoes in a dark place as light causes greening and a bitter taste. This greening, caused by solanine, is mildly poisonous and if eaten may cause a headache or an upset stomach. There is no danger of poisoning from these potatoes, however, if the green areas are removed.

High temperatures may cause sprouting and shriveling. Potatoes stored at room temperature should be used within a week.

Potatoes should never be stored in the refrigerator. Too cool temperatures will cause the starch in the potato to turn to sugar and give the potato an undesirable sweet taste. Potatoes that are too cold will also darken when cooked.

If possible, store potatoes in bins raised slightly from the floor to permit air to circulate. Potatoes are living and breathing. They must have air. Never store in a plastic bag or closed container.

If stored properly, potatoes will keep several months.

Potato Varieties

Potatoes are available in a variety of colors, shapes, and textures. The potato's appearance is related to its use. For example, long potatoes are best for baking, while round potatoes are best for boiling. This chart shows some of Canada's more widely used varieties.

Type	Variety
Russets	Russet Burbank (Netted Gem)
Round whites	Kennebec
	Sebago
	Superior
Reds	Chieftain
Yellow-fleshed	Bintje

Appearance and Texture	*Uses*
Oblong, slightly flattened lengthwise; lightly russeted, buff skin; white flesh; shallow eyes, fluffy texture produces light quality.	Best for mashed, baked, broiled, and French fried potatoes; also in baked goods.
Round; smooth white skin; white flesh; slower to discolor than most other varieties so are most suitable when working with raw potatoes.	An all-purpose potato, best for boiled, baked, and French fried potatoes.
Round; smooth ivory-yellow skin; white flesh; a waxy potato that keeps its shape.	Best for boiling and in salads.
Round; smooth, white skin with a light flaky russet; white flesh.	Best for boiling.
Round; smooth bright-red skin; white flesh.	Best for boiling.
Long oval-shaped; large; smooth, pale yellow skin, shallow eyes; light yellow flesh.	Best for boiling, baking, French fries, and potato chips.

Potato By-products

Potato starch is preferred by some cooks, rather than flour, as a thickener in sauces. When it is used, less simmering is required. However, it has no holding power, so foods thickened with potato starch must be served soon after thickening. One tablespoon of potato starch will thicken 1 cup of liquid to a moderate thickness.

Potato flour is a fine white flour made from cooked, dried potatoes. It is often used as a thickener in soups, sauces, and stews. Potato flour has a taste of its own and should not be substituted for all-purpose flour. It can be used in breads, it can be mixed with another flour that has an adequate gluten content, or it can be used in some cakes and crackers for people on gluten-free diets.

Potato cheese is a German cheese made from cow's milk or occasionally sheep's or goat's milk. The milk is allowed to form a curd, then is added to boiled sieved potatoes along with salt and sometimes caraway seed. Cheeses are shaped, dried, and covered with beer or cream before being set to ripen for 2 weeks.

The potato chip is one potato dish that is truly American. It is said to have been invented by a Native American, George Crum, of the Adirondack tribe. Crum was a chef at a popular spa, Moon's Lake House, at Saratoga Springs, New York, in the mid-nineteenth century. Legend tells us he became upset when customers complained of the thickness of his fried potatoes. He cut the next batch paper thin with his razor. Whether this is true or not, the potato chip, originally called "Saratoga Chip," was born and today is North America's most popular snack food.

Potato chips are paper-thin slices of potato, soaked in cold water, then deep-fried in oil. They are then drained, seasoned, and packaged. One store in New Hampshire devotes 3 entire aisles to various flavored potato chips.

In the early 1960s, Premier Nikita Khrushchev of Russia was served potato chips on an American airplane. He then had a memo printed in *Pravda* in 1963, telling about the potato chip.

Potato Ice Cream is an all-natural sugar-free dairy product developed by Alan Reed of Idaho. In this new and innovative product, potato flakes are used as a stabilizing agent, and apple concentrate acts as the natural sweetener. Prince Edward Island businessmen Jack and Wes Sheridan are now attempting to produce Potato Ice Cream on the Island. Because the recipe has been written for mass quantities only, we are unable to include it here.

The International Potato Centre

The International Potato Centre, herein called CIP from its Spanish name *Centro Internacional de La Papa,* is the hub of the world's potato research. The CIP, situated just outside Lima, Peru, is a non-profit scientific institution established in 1971 with the agreement of the government of Peru. It is funded by several foreign governments, regional organizations, and private institutions, under the sponsorship of the World Bank. The goal of the CIP is "to develop improved agricultural technology, to increase food production and to improve the welfare of poor people in developing countries."

There are approximately 400 people employed at the institute with several foreign anthropologists among the staff. The activities of the institute focus on research, training, and dissemination of information on the potato. The center has the world's most extensive collection of potato cultivars and exports seed tubers, seedlings, true potato seed, and tissue culture to some 80 countries.

One of the programs from CIP, supported by the government of Ireland, provides a dry-food mix, made from three-tenths mashed potatoes combined with a mixture of available grains and legumes, that is given to school children as a dietary supplement. This mixture can be served in various ways, including a form of dessert.

The emblem of the CIP is a pre-Columbian deity holding a potato plant in each hand—one healthy and the other unhealthy. In 1981 a stamp was issued to commemorate the tenth anniversary of the center.

Some of the recipes in this book have been adapted from a book compiled and published in 1978 by the CIP Women's Club. The book, written in both Spanish and English, is entitled *International Potato Cookery.*

The Potato Museum, Washington, D.C.

There are over 25,000 museums around the world, yet, until 1975, none was dedicated solely to the potato.

Tom Hughes is founder and director of the world's first Potato Museum. He and his wife Meredith are curators of what *The New Yorker* called "one of the world's most exotic institutions."

Tom started the Potato Museum in Belgium in 1975 when he was employed as a fifth-grade teacher at the International School in Brussels. The museum grew steadily and in 1983 was moved to the United States. It is now situated in the Hughes' home on Capitol Hill, at 704 North Carolina Avenue, S.E., Washington, D.C.

The museum's collection now numbers over 2500 items, all of which cannot be displayed at once. However, the museum is open by appointment and visitors will find a fascinating variety of items on view. Included are songs, poems, books, and major articles written about the potato, as well as ancient potato digging tools, mashers, and peelers. There are bottles of potato liquors, toys, jewelry, postage stamps, and even an 1828 "wanted" poster telling of a scoundrel from New Hampshire who stole a potato still. These and many more items form part of the world's most extensive collection of potato folklore.

A brochure from the museum states, "the museum aims to educate and entertain the public about this valuable plant while preserving items associated with its history and social influence."

Funding for the museum comes from $20 memberships which include a subscription to *Peelings,* the monthly newsletter. As well as editing the newsletter, Meredith Hughes spends much time in the museum kitchen trying recipes for "Potato Eaters' Night," which is a Wednesday night smorgasbord of potato dishes shared with friends. The museum is not funded with government assistance. The Hughes believe that one way of generating additional funding could be to open these dinners to the public.

THE POTATO COOKBOOK

Helpful Hints

A teaspoon of grated raw potato in a compress of surgical gauze is said to smooth eyelid wrinkles when placed over the closed eye for 15 minutes.

To soften and remove blemishes from hands, make a paste from 1 medium cooked mashed potato, 1 tbsp. safflower oil, and a few drops of rose water. Apply to the hands, leave for 30 minutes, and wash off. (This tip came to me from a penpal in Tasmania.)

Tired of oily skin? Blend ¼ cup potatoes, peeled and grated, 1 egg white, and 1 tbsp. dry milk powder. Apply mixture to clean face. Leave 20 to 30 minutes. Wash off with warm water.

Raw potato is an old folk cure for cleansing the skin. "Rub a raw peeled potato on the skin directly or drink the juice regularly. This will cure eczema. Extract the juice with a liquidizer and mix with equal amounts of carrot juice to make it more palatable. Drink a glass a day." -Margaret Faulkner, Tasmania. (I have not tried the juice, but I have used raw potato to remove vegetable stains from my hands.)

A slice of raw potato will clean wood and silver.

A fun and simple activity for children is making potato prints. Cut a potato in half with a sharp knife. Carve out a picture or design, then dip in colored ink and press on paper or fabric. Using paper grocery bags or inexpensive newsprint, children can make their own personalized gift wrap.

Don't throw away vitamins and minerals! Use leftover potato water in sauces, soups, or baked goods.

¼ tsp. cream of tartar added to the cooking water for the last 10 minutes will prevent potatoes from turning dark.

Too much salt in the soup? Add more potato. Simmer 30 minutes and discard the extra spuds.

Try adding mashed potatoes to your favorite recipes. Start by adding ½ cup to drop cookies, biscuits, fruit loaves, or muffins. Potatoes help retain moisture in baked goods.

To thicken soups, add 3 tbsp. grated raw potato for each cup of soup and simmer about 15 minutes.

The best method of cooking potatoes to preserve the maximum mineral content and taste is to bake them in hot coals or in the oven.

Don't waste potato peelings. The cortex of the potato, just below the skin, holds one-third of the potato's nutrients. If you must peel potatoes, peel them thinly.

Boiling potatoes in too much water or overcooking them will cause them to break up.

Baking potatoes without pricking the skin can cause an explosion in your oven.

Potatoes can be baked at 425 degrees for 40 to 50 minutes, at 375 degrees for 50 to 60 minutes, or at 325 degrees for 75 minutes. Bake potatoes along with whatever else you may have in the oven.

Raw potatoes should never be stored in the refrigerator. Temperatures below 40 degrees will cause the starch in potatoes to convert to sugar. This produces an undesirable sweet flavor in cooked potatoes.

Try sprinkling some dry milk powder in a little potato water and add it to the potatoes as you mash them. Fast, economical, and nutritious . . . and creamy mashed potatoes.

Potatoes begin to turn green when exposed to light—both sunlight and artificial light. To prevent this, store potatoes in a cool, dark place.

Remove all green areas found on potatoes before cooking. This green causes a bitter flavor in cooked potatoes and is mildly poisonous, often resulting in an upset stomach.

Potatoes can be baked in a covered coffee can or on an asbestos pad on top of a stove.

Too much fat on top of soup or gravy? Drop in a few large cold potato slices. The fat will cling to the cold potatoes which can then be discarded.

After deep frying, purify your fat by adding some thick slices of raw potato. Any taste of doughnuts, fish, or onion, for example, will be absorbed by the potato, leaving the fat clear for the next time you use it.

If you burn your potatoes, scrape off the burnt part and put them in another pot. Add cold water and a speck of lemon juice and cook a few minutes longer. The burnt taste will be gone.

Is your sauce too thin? Add 1 tbsp. potato starch and ½ cup cold water.

Add diced pimento to hot mashed potatoes for color.

To keep mashed potatoes hot, cover and place the dish in a skillet of hot water.

Potatoes, unpeeled and boiled in salted water, do not absorb salt the way peeled potatoes do . . . important in some diets.

Potatoes that are boiled for about 5 minutes before baking will bake in half the usual time. Baking a potato with an aluminum skewer through it also cuts cooking time in half. (Don't try this method in a microwave though!)

Try oiling the skin of a potato before you bake it. The skins will be delicious.

To slice potatoes thinly, dip knife blade in boiling water.

To prevent potatoes from turning dark when peeled, put them in slightly salted water until ready to use. Or, add ascorbic acid to raw potatoes; dissolve 2-100 mg. tablets of ascorbic acid in 2 tbsp. water for each cup of potatoes.

For a new taste, cook potatoes in beef or chicken broth.

Prepare a "trim potato" scallop by replacing the whole milk with skim milk or broth.

For lower calories with baked potatoes, try a "Mock Sour Cream." Combine 1 cup cottage cheese, 1 tbsp. lemon juice, and ¼ cup water. Add salt to taste. Blend well.

APPETIZERS

For your next festive occasion, serve a variety of hot and cold appetizers: colorful dainties that are pleasing in texture and taste. As the beginning of a fancy luncheon or a pleasant ending to an evening out, appetizers are special "little somethings" that assure your friends you are glad they came. Served informally as help-yourself snacks, they can put your guests at ease.

Appetizers excite the appetite and set the stage for the meal to come. Try a "potato specialty" at your next party. The recipes included here are suitable for all occasions.

Note: The potato is the only vegetable to have a war named after it. That war was the Kartoffel Kreig (kartoffel = potato; kreig = war) of 1778-1779, also known as the War of the Bavarian Succession. Frederick the Great of Prussia was at odds with Austria. The armies ate one another's potatoes and, when cold weather set in, the fighting had to stop.

THE POTATO COOKBOOK

CRISP POTATO SKINS

Potato skins are fast becoming a popular snack food. They make an easy appetizer that is well worth trying. They're also great with soup.

6 medium baked potatoes or skins from leftover baked potatoes
½ cup melted butter or margarine
1 tsp. garlic salt, celery salt, or any desired seasoning salt
¼ cup grated parmesan or Swiss cheese

Preheat oven to 350 degrees. Cut baked potatoes into quarters. Scoop out pulp,* leaving only a thin layer of potato on each skin. Place skin side down on a baking sheet and brush well with melted butter. Sprinkle with desired seasoning salt. Bake for 20 to 25 minutes until skins are brown and crisp. Sprinkle with cheese for the last 5 minutes of cooking period. Serve hot. Serves 2 to 4.

*Save the potato pulp for hash browns or mash and use in any one of the many baked products.

Note: Before putting in the oven, any of the following toppings may be added:
1. 3 strips bacon, cooked crisp and crumbled, mixed with ¼ cup grated cheddar cheese.
2. Equal amounts grated onion and green pepper, sautéed until tender in melted butter.
3. Fresh mushrooms, sliced and brushed with butter.

Note: Potatoes were planted in the Berlin Lustgarten in 1651 as an ornamental flower by Frederick the Great Elector. His grandson, Frederick William I, was convinced that potatoes had great nutritive value. He threatened to have the noses and ears cut off any of his subjects who refused to plant them.

POTATO CHEESE PUFFS

This is an attractive, tempting potato dish.

2 beaten egg yolks
1⅓ cups mashed potato
3 tbsp. hot milk
⅓ cup grated cheddar cheese
¼ tsp. salt
¼ tsp. paprika
¼ tsp. celery salt
½ tsp. finely minced onion
1 tsp. chopped green pepper
2 stiffly beaten egg whites
1½ tbsp. melted butter or margarine

Preheat oven to 350 degrees. Combine egg yolks, potato, milk, cheese, salt, paprika, celery salt, onion, and green pepper. Mix well. Fold in beaten egg whites. Drop in mounds on a greased cookie sheet. Brush with melted butter. Bake for 20 minutes. Serve hot. Makes 24 puffs; serves 6 to 8.

POTATO LEMON STICKS

4 medium potatoes, unpeeled and cut in quarters
2 tsp. lemon juice
2 tsp. melted butter or margarine
2 tsp. finely grated lemon peel
3 tbsp. grated parmesan cheese
Paprika

Preheat oven to 400 degrees. Mix together lemon juice and butter and brush on cut sides of the potato quarters. Combine lemon peel and cheese. Sprinkle over potatoes. Sprinkle with paprika. Place on a baking sheet. Bake for 30 to 35 minutes until potatoes are tender. Serve hot. Serves 4 to 6.

CANDIED NEW POTATOES

This is a popular dish in China and Denmark.

18 to 20 medium new potatoes (not as large as mature potatoes)
½ cup brown sugar, packed
¼ cup water
2 tbsp. butter or margarine
1 tsp. salt
1 tbsp. fresh dill

Boil and peel potatoes. Combine sugar, water, butter, and salt. Cook over medium heat, stirring constantly until slightly thickened and bubbly. Reduce heat and stir in dill. Add potatoes and cook for 10 to 15 minutes. Stir potatoes in syrup to be sure they are evenly coated. They should glisten and be a rich brown color. Serve hot. Serves 6 to 8.

PARTY POTATO PUFFS

The potatoes for this recipe should be at room temperature. If they are not soft, add a little milk or water and beat.

1 cup mashed potato
½ cup sifted all-purpose flour
1 tsp. double-acting baking powder
¼ tsp. salt
1 slightly beaten egg
1 tsp. parsley flakes
Fat for pan frying (385 degrees)

Combine potato, flour, baking powder, and salt. Add egg and parsley. Mix well. Drop by half-teaspoons into hot fat. Fry to a golden brown. Drain on absorbent paper. Serve hot. Makes about 3 dozen appetizers.

MEXICAN POTATO PUFFS

These delicious appetizers may be made ahead and frozen for up to a month.

3 cups mashed potato
3 beaten eggs
1 tsp. chili powder
⅛ tsp. cayenne pepper
1 tsp. salt
½ tsp. dry mustard
1 tbsp. grated onion
2 tsp. milk
¾ cup grated cheddar cheese
¾ cup dry bread crumbs
Fat for deep frying (400 to 450 degrees)

Combine all ingredients except cheese and bread crumbs. Chop cheese and crumbs in blender until fine. Add 1 cup to potato mixture. Shape in balls using one rounded tablespoon for each. Roll in remaining crumb mixture. Deep fry until golden brown. Serve hot. Makes 48 puffs; serves 10 to 12.

POTATO PEEL PICKS

4 medium potatoes
1 egg white
Salt and pepper
Dash of onion powder, garlic powder, and oregano
2 tbsp. parmesan cheese

Preheat oven to 475 degrees. Peel potatoes with fairly thick peels. Cut peels in 2" slivers. Brush with egg white. Sprinkle with seasonings and roll in cheese. Bake on a greased cookie sheet for 10 minutes. Toss to make crisp on all sides. Serve hot. Serves 4 to 6.

THE POTATO COOKBOOK

POMMES DAUPHINE

This is an original Jewish recipe despite the French name.

3 cups warm mashed potato
⅔ cup butter or margarine
¼ cup whipping cream
2 beaten egg yolks
1 cup water
1¼ tsp. salt
1 cup all-purpose flour
4 eggs
Fat for deep frying (370 degrees)

Combine potato with 4 tbsp. butter, cream, egg yolks, and 1 tsp. salt. In a saucepan heat water, remaining butter, and ¼ tsp. salt until butter is melted and mixture is boiling rapidly. Add flour all at once. Remove pan from the heat and stir in flour quickly. Hold pan above the heat and stir mixture until the dough is thick and pulls away from the sides of the pan to form a ball. Remove from heat. Add the eggs, one at a time, beating well after each addition. Add potato and beat in well. Drop by teaspoon into fat. Cook until they are lightly browned and puffed. Drain on paper towels. Serve hot or cold. Serves 8.

Note: The Indians of pre-Columbian Peru sometimes buried potato-shaped stones in their potato beds to encourage regeneration.

POTATO CROQUETTES

This basic recipe has variations.

2 cups finely mashed potato
2 tbsp. butter or margarine
½ tsp. salt
⅛ tsp. pepper
Dash cayenne pepper
2 egg yolks
¼ tsp. celery salt
1 tsp. fresh chopped parsley

Combine all ingredients. Mix until soft and creamy. Chill 15 to 20 minutes to make easier to handle. Shape in balls by rolling one rounded tablespoon of mixture in handshape into a log shape.

Note: Egg and Crumb Variation: Dip logs in a mixture of one beaten egg and 2 tbsp. water. Coat with 1 cup sifted bread crumbs. Deep fry in fat at 390 degrees. Serve hot. Serves 4.

Potato Apples Variation: Prepare croquettes, omitting pepper. Add 2 tbsp. cream, ⅓ cup grated cheddar cheese, and a dash of nutmeg. Shape like small apples. Roll in flour, then beaten egg, then sifted crumbs. Deep fry as above. Insert clove at stem end of each croquette. Serve hot. Serves 6.

HEATED HERBED POTATO CHIPS

Preheat oven to 350 degrees. Spread potato chips on a cookie sheet. Top with shredded cheddar cheese. Sprinkle lightly with thyme, marjoram, or basil. Heat for 5 minutes, until cheese melts. Serve hot.

POTATO BASKETS

These dainty baskets are served with any desired filling. Creamed vegetables or fish are especially tasty.

3 cups hot mashed potato
1 tsp. salt
3 tbsp. butter or margarine
3 egg yolks, slightly beaten
2 tbsp. milk or cream
1 egg white, slightly beaten

Preheat oven to 350 degrees. Combine potato, salt, butter, egg yolks, and milk. Blend well. Shape into small baskets on greased cookie sheet, using a pastry bag and tube or a spoon. Brush with egg white and brown in oven. Fill while hot with desired filling. Makes 12 baskets; serves 6.

FILLING

2 tbsp. butter or margarine
2 tbsp. all-purpose flour
1 cup milk
Salt to taste
Chopped meat, flaked fish, or cooked vegetables

Melt butter; stir in flour and salt. Gradually add milk. Cook over medium heat, stirring constantly until thickened. Add meat, fish, or vegetables. Heat thoroughly.

Note: People of medieval Europe believed a potato in your pocket would prevent rheumatism. They thought that pregnant women who ate potatoes at night would give birth to children with large heads. They also believed that the placing of a potato skin at a young lady's door was an expression of contempt.

DEEP-FRIED POTATO APPLES

**Tiny new potatoes (size of crab apples) or potato balls made
with a melon scoop
Whole cloves
Parsley
Paprika
Fat for deep frying (375 degrees)**

Peel small potatoes. Soak in cold water for 15 minutes. Parboil 2 minutes and pat dry. Fry as for French fries. Insert a clove to represent the blossom end of an apple and put a sprig of parsley in the other end for a stem. Dust with paprika. Serve hot.

SALT COD AND POTATO NIBBLERS

This recipe for these tasty bite-sized nibblers comes from the Prince Edward Island Department of Fisheries.

**1 lb. salt cod
2 tbsp. melted butter or margarine
3 cups mashed potato
1 tbsp. lemon juice
2/3 tsp. onion salt
1/4 tsp. pepper
1/4 tsp. garlic salt
1 beaten egg
Crushed cracker crumbs**

Soak fish in cold water overnight. Boil in fresh water for 20 minutes. Drain and flake. Preheat oven to 450 degrees. Blend melted butter well with potato, fish, lemon juice, onion salt, pepper, and garlic salt. Form into party balls and dampen with beaten egg. Roll in crushed cracker crumbs. Place on a well-greased baking sheet. Bake for 8 to 10 minutes or until browned and heated through. Serve hot. Makes 36 nibblers.

POTATO FRITTERS

2 cups hot mashed potato
2 tbsp. white wine
2 tbsp. cream
1 tsp. salt
Shake of nutmeg
3 well-beaten eggs
2 well-beaten egg yolks
½ cup all-purpose flour
Dash cayenne pepper
Fat for deep frying (375 degrees)

Combine potato, wine, cream, salt, and nutmeg. Add eggs and egg yolks; place bowl in a larger bowl of iced water. Beat until cold. Add flour and cayenne pepper; mix well. Dip a metal spoon into hot fat, then spoon fritter batter into fat. Cook only 3 to 4 fritters at a time. Cook 3 to 5 minutes, until a delicate brown color. Drain on absorbent paper. Serve hot. Serves 8.

POTATO-ROMA SNACKS

5 to 6 medium potatoes, boiled and mashed
2 egg yolks
½ cup grated parmesan cheese
2 tbsp. vegetable oil
2 tbsp. chopped onion
¼ cup chopped fresh parsley
1 tsp. salt
1 tsp. garlic salt
½ tsp. pepper
¾ cup all-purpose flour
2 beaten eggs
1 cup fine dry bread crumbs
Fat for deep frying (375 degrees)

Add egg yolks and cheese to mashed potato. Mix well. Sauté onion in oil until tender. Add to potato mixture; stir in parsley, salt, garlic salt, and pepper. Stir until smooth. Shape into small balls (1 rounded tsp. for each ball). Roll in flour, dip in egg, then roll in bread crumbs. Deep fry until brown in hot oil. Snacks may be refrigerated, or frozen and thawed at room temperature, then reheated in a slow oven. Serve hot. Serves 6 to 8.

CINDY'S PARTY SNACKS

Cindy Chase of Halifax shared this recipe with me.

2 cups hot mashed potato
2 tbsp. chopped mint leaves
¼ tsp. paprika
½ tsp. salt
2 tbsp. butter or margarine
1 egg yolk
1 egg white, slightly beaten
2 tbsp. water
1 cup sifted bread crumbs
Fat for deep frying (350 degrees)

Combine potato, mint, paprika, salt, butter, and egg yolk. Shape in small balls. Dilute slightly beaten egg white with 2 tbsp. water. Dip balls in liquid. Roll in crumbs and deep fry until brown. Serve hot. Makes approximately 24 party snacks.

Note: Frederick the Great of Prussia believed the best time for planting potatoes was in the dark of the moon.

THE POTATO COOKBOOK

POTATO AND FISH TIDBITS

Use whatever fish you have on hand. Potatoes blend equally well with cod, blue-fish, and salmon, to name a few.

1 lb. cooked fish, drained and flaked
3 cups mashed potato
2 tbsp. melted butter or margarine
1 small onion, very finely chopped
1 tsp. salt
¼ tsp. pepper
1 tbsp. lemon juice
1 beaten egg
1 cup dry bread crumbs (approx.)
Fat for deep frying (350 degrees)

Combine fish, potato, butter, onion, salt, pepper, and lemon juice. Mix well. Form into bite-sized balls. Dip in beaten egg and roll in bread crumbs. Deep fry in fat for 2 to 3 minutes. Drain on absorbent paper. Serve hot. Serves 10 to 12.

SALMON-POTATO MINI PUFFS

2 egg whites
2 egg yolks
1 small can salmon (8-oz.)
1½ cups mashed potato
2 tbsp. mayonnaise
1 tbsp. chopped fresh parsley
¼ tsp. lemon rind
Salt and pepper to taste
Dash of onion salt

Preheat oven to 375 degrees. Beat egg whites to stiff peaks and set aside. Combine all other ingredients. Fold in egg whites. Spoon tablespoons of batter into small balls. Set in a shallow pan of water and oven poach for 20 minutes. Serve hot. Serves 6 to 8.

MINI SEAFOOD QUICHES

1 recipe potato pastry
1 cup canned mackerel
¼ cup finely chopped onion
1 cup grated Swiss cheese
2 beaten eggs
1 cup light cream
2 tbsp. parsley flakes
½ tsp. salt
Pinch of pepper
Paprika

Preheat oven to 350 degrees. Prepare pastry. Roll out and cut into circles for lining muffin tins. Drain fish and flake into a bowl. Combine onion and cheese. Fill tart shells ⅔ full with mackerel mixture. Beat eggs, cream, parsley, salt, and pepper until well-blended. Spoon egg mixture into each tart shell being careful not to fill too full. Sprinkle with paprika. Bake for 40 minutes until a knife inserted in the center comes out clean. Serve hot. Makes 12 mini quiches.

Note: How did potatoes, one of the world's great health-giving foods, get the name "spud"? One story goes that when potatoes were first introduced in Europe, the mainstay of life was grain. The large milling industry, fearful of competition from potatoes, did everything possible to discourage the consumption of potatoes. They organized societies to dissuade people from eating the new tubers. The groups were called "The Society to Prevent Unhealthy Diets": hence, "spud."

BREAKFASTS

Want something different for breakfast? Why not serve potatoes? Potatoes combine well with a variety of ingredients to make delicious and nutritious breakfasts. Pancakes, soufflés, omelettes and quiche are just a few of the tempting potato breakfasts you'll find in this chapter.

Note: A Scandinavian man lived healthily for 300 days on potatoes and a small amount of butter.

THE POTATO COOKBOOK

POTATO FARMER'S BREAKFAST

¼ lb. bacon
3 cups cubed cooked potato
1 cup chopped onion
2 tbsp. chopped chives
6 eggs, beaten
½ tsp. salt
¼ tsp. pepper
½ cup grated cheddar cheese

Fry bacon in a large frying pan. Drain fat. Add cubed potato, onion, and chives. Cook 5 minutes. Stir in beaten eggs, salt, and pepper. Sprinkle grated cheese over mixture. Cover and cook over moderate heat for an additional 5 minutes. Cut in wedges to serve. Serves 6.

GERMAN WINTERLAND DELIGHT

This is a quick, satisfying breakfast or supper dish.

6 slices bacon
2 tbsp. chopped onion
3 large boiled potatoes, cubed
Salt and pepper to taste
6 eggs
Grated cheese (optional)

Fry bacon over low heat until brown and crisp; cut into small pieces. Fry onion, potatoes, bacon, salt, and pepper in bacon fat and cook until potatoes are browned. Stir often. Break eggs into pan over top of potatoes. Cover and cook over low heat until eggs are set. Sprinkle with grated cheese if desired, either before or after eggs are added. Serve hot. Serves 6.

SAVORY COUNTRY-STYLE SCRAMBLE

Potatoes team up with bacon and eggs for a special brunch. Serve with tomato slices and green beans.

3 slices bacon
1 tbsp. oil
2 cups diced raw potato
¼ cup chopped onion
⅛ tsp. savory
4 eggs
1 tbsp. water
¼ tsp. salt
Dash pepper
¼ cup diced cheese

Fry bacon in large frying pan, retaining drippings. Crumble and set aside. Add oil, potato, onion, and savory to bacon drippings. Cover and cook over low heat, stirring frequently, until potato is tender (approximately 30 minutes). Stir in crumbled bacon. Blend eggs, water, salt, and pepper. Pour over the potato mixture and cover. When partially set, lift and turn in sections. Sprinkle cheese on top; cover and cook for 3 minutes or until cheese is melted. Serve at once. Serves 4.

Note: Many people rejected potatoes because they "wanted no truck with anything that grew underground."

In 1619 the potato was banned in Burgundy, France. It was believed to cause leprosy, a misconception that lasted well into the eighteenth century.

BAKED EGGS IN POTATO BOATS

This makes a great breakfast as well as an easy lunch on a lazy day.

3 large baked potatoes
3 tbsp. butter
½ tsp. salt
⅛ tsp. pepper
¼ cup hot milk
6 eggs

Preheat oven to 350 degrees. Cut potatoes in half lengthwise and scoop out pulp. Be careful not to break the potato skins. Mash potatoes; add butter, salt, pepper, and milk. Beat until light and fluffy. Spoon into potato shells, leaving a hollow in each. Break an egg in each hollow. Season with additional salt and pepper if desired, and bake until eggs are firm. Serves 6.

SAUCY EGG AND POTATO PATTIES

2 cups mashed potato
Salt and pepper to taste
¼ cup grated cheddar cheese
Butter or margarine for frying
1½ cups cooked tomato
¼ cup chopped onion
6 eggs

Combine potato, salt, pepper, and cheese. Shape mixture into 6 patties and brown in skillet in butter. Cook tomato and onion until thick. Fry eggs and place one egg on each potato patty. Cover with tomato sauce. Serve at once. Make 6 servings.

FISHERMAN'S DELIGHT

A great breakfast at home or on your next camping trip, it tastes especially good if you are lucky enough to have fresh trout.

4 well-beaten eggs
1 cup milk
1 cup mashed potato
1 cup all-purpose flour
1 small onion, finely chopped
Fat for frying

Mix all ingredients. Pour in just enough batter to barely cover bottom of frying pan. Cook a few minutes and turn over as you would pancakes. Serve with maple syrup and bacon, sausage, or trout. Serves 4.

CHEESY POTATO SOUFFLE

2 cups mashed potato, slightly cooled
4 slices cooked ham, cut in small cubes
½ cup grated cheddar cheese
6 egg yolks
½ tsp. salt
Pinch pepper
6 egg whites

Preheat oven to 325 degrees. Combine mashed potato, ham, and cheese; mix well. Beat egg yolks, add to potato mixture. Stir in salt and pepper; beat until light and fluffy. In a large bowl, beat egg whites until they form stiff peaks. Gently fold egg whites into potato mixture. Place in a 1½-quart ungreased casserole and bake for 25 minutes, until puffed and golden brown. Serve at once. Makes 6 servings.

MEAT-AND-POTATO QUICHE

This is an attractive dish with its browned crispy potato edging.

3 tbsp. vegetable oil
3 cups coarsely grated raw potato
1 cup grated cheddar or Swiss cheese
¾ cup cooked diced meat (ham, chicken, or sausage)
¼ cup chopped onion
1 cup evaporated milk
2 eggs
⅓ tsp. salt
⅛ tsp. pepper
1 tbsp. parsley flakes

Preheat oven to 425 degrees. Combine vegetable oil and grated potato. Press evenly into a 9" pie plate to form a pie crust. Bake for 15 minutes until it begins to brown. Remove from oven. Cover potato crust with cheese, meat, and onion in layers. Mix together milk, eggs, salt, and pepper. Pour over other ingredients. Sprinkle with parsley. Bake 30 minutes until knife inserted in center comes out clean. Cool 5 minutes before cutting. Serves 6.

POTATO OMELETTE

What a delightful way to start the day!

3 egg yolks
3 tbsp. cream
1 cup mashed potato
1 tsp. salt
¼ tsp. pepper
1 tbsp. finely grated onion
Chopped fresh parsley
3 egg whites
Butter

Preheat oven to 350 degrees. Combine egg yolks, cream, and potato; beat until smooth. Season to taste with salt, pepper, grated onion, and parsley. Beat egg whites until stiff. Fold into potato mixture. Place in a buttered casserole dish or skillet. Bake until brown (approximately 10 to 15 minutes). Fold and turn onto a hot serving platter. Serve at once. Serves 4 to 6.

Note: The word "boycott" came from the time when Captain Boycott's tenants refused to dig potatoes and other crops for him. Their rebellion was on September 22, 1873.

THE POTATO COOKBOOK

POTATO PEPPERONI OMELETTE

This omelette takes a bit longer to make than most. Try it for a Sunday brunch and enjoy a taste of Spain. Prepare omelettes in a large electric frying pan or any covered frying pan.

2 tbsp. butter or margarine
2 tbsp. olive oil
1¼ cups finely diced raw potato
½ cup chopped Spanish onion
½ cup sliced mushrooms
1 clove garlic, minced
8 eggs
Salt to taste
Dash crushed red pepper
½ cup chopped pepperoni

Heat butter and oil over medium heat. Add potato and cook until tender, about 15 minutes. Stir often to distribute heat evenly. Add onion, mushrooms, and garlic. Cook another few minutes until tender. Beat eggs, salt, and pepper; combine with pepperoni. Add to the vegetable mixture. Cover and cook 4 to 5 minutes until slightly set. Flip omelette and cook other side for another 4 minutes. Serve hot. Serves 8.

Note: The Inca Indians measured time by how long it took potatoes to cook.

GRATED-POTATO PANCAKES

        3 cups raw potato, grated
        2 eggs, beaten
        1 cup milk
        ½ cup finely minced onion
        ¼ cup all-purpose flour
        2 tsp. baking powder
        1 tsp. salt
        Fat for frying

Drain liquid from grated potato. Combine eggs, milk, and onion. Sift dry ingredients and add to mixture. Fold in potato. Melt a little fat in a skillet and cook pancakes in ⅓ cup amounts. Brown on both sides, turning once. Serve hot with applesauce. Makes 10 pancakes.

"Tu me dices papas." -A Spanish expression meaning "you're fibbing" or, literally translated, "you are telling me potatoes."

POTATO PANCAKES I

Made with leftover mashed potato, these quickly prepared pancakes are a family favorite at our house.

        1 cup mashed potato
        2 cups sifted all-purpose flour
        1 tsp. salt
        3 tsp. baking powder
        1 tsp. nutmeg
        2 eggs, beaten
        1 cup milk (approx.)
        ¼ cup light corn syrup

Combine potato, sifted flour, salt, baking powder, and nutmeg. Mix together eggs and milk; stir lightly into potato-flour mixture. Add corn syrup and beat well. If batter is too thick you may need to add a bit more milk. Brown on both sides on a greased griddle, turning once. Serve with Potato Maple Syrup (see Miscellaneous). Serves 6.

POTATO PANCAKES II

These pancakes are served with ham, sausage, bacon, or eggs for breakfast or brunch. They can be accompanied by sour cream, maple syrup, applesauce, or any desired pancake topping.

3 cups grated raw potato
6 tbsp. milk
3 tbsp. all-purpose flour
¼ tsp. baking power
1 egg
1 small onion, grated finely
1 tsp. salt
Fat for greasing skillet

Combine all ingredients except fat. Pour in small amounts on a hot greased skillet. Brown on both sides, turning once. Serves 6.

PERUVIAN POTATO PANCAKES

A recipe for a big family breakfast, this makes light and fluffy pancakes. Serve with Potato Maple Syrup (see Miscellaneous).

1½ cups all-purpose flour
1 cup mashed potato
5 tsp. baking powder
1 tsp. salt
3 tbsp. granulated sugar
2 eggs
2 cups milk
⅓ cup oil
Fat for frying

Preheat a large frying pan (if using an electric one, heat to 375 degrees). Put all ingredients in a blender. Mix only until smooth and free of lumps. Do not overmix. (I find putting the liquid ingredients in first makes a better batter.) Grease frying pan lightly and cook pancakes in ¼ cup amounts. When top side of pancake bubbles, turn over and brown other side. Serve hot. Makes 30 pancakes.

POTATO-CARROT PANCAKES

4 eggs
2 cups raw potato, finely grated
2 cups raw carrot, finely grated
1 tbsp. onion, chopped
2 tbsp. all-purpose flour
1¼ tsp. salt
¼ tsp. baking powder
¼ tsp. dill seed (optional)
Oil for frying

Beat eggs. Add potato, carrot, onion, and dry ingredients. Mix thoroughly. Pour in ¼ cup portions on moderately hot frying pan. Flatten with spatula. Fry until crisp and browned; turn and cook until other side is browned. If necessary, drain pancakes on paper towel. Add oil to pan before making each set of pancakes. Serve hot with sour cream. Serves 6.

HOLIDAY POTATO PANCAKES

A potato pancake with a difference: finely chopped cooked turkey is added to the batter. Pancakes can be served with cranberry sauce. Makes a special Boxing Day brunch.

3 medium grated raw potatoes (about 2½ cups)
1 tsp. salt
Dash pepper
2 eggs, beaten
2 tbsp. all-purpose flour
1 tbsp. finely chopped onion
1 cup finely chopped cooked turkey
Fat for frying

Combine all ingredients. Drop by spoonfuls on lightly oiled hot skillet. Fry until brown on one side, then turn and brown other side. Serve hot with cranberry sauce or maple syrup. Serves 4 to 6.

OLD SOUTH POTATO CORN PUDDING

Canned corn gives a new twist to leftover potatoes. This popular quiche-like Sunday brunch dish is ready in just 30 minutes.

1 tbsp. butter or margarine
2 cups cooked potato, cut in small cubes
2 green onions, sliced (use entire onion)
1 cup whole kernel corn, drained
¾ tsp. salt
½ tsp. thyme
¼ tsp. pepper
1¼ cups milk
2 eggs, beaten
Paprika

Preheat oven to 375 degrees. Melt butter to sizzling in large pan. Add potato and onion. Cook and stir for 5 minutes. Mix in corn, salt, thyme, pepper, and milk. Remove from heat. Stir in eggs until thoroughly blended. Pour into a greased 9" pie plate or quiche dish. Dust with paprika. Bake 15 to 18 minutes, until set. Cut in wedges to serve. Leftovers may be refrigerated and served chilled or reheated in a microwave oven. Serves 4 to 6.

"(The potato) . . . a fode, as also a meate for pleasure, . . . being either rosted in the embers, or boiled and eaten with oile, vinegar, and pepper, or dressed any other way by the hand of come cunning cookerie." *-John Berarde, 1597*

QUICK BREADS

The nicest thing about quick breads is just that—they are quick. For a special breakfast, when unexpected guests drop in, or to share when a friend has a problem, quick breads say without words, "I made something special just for you."

Quick breads are leavened with baking powder, baking soda, and eggs rather than yeast (leaving a distinctive crack down the center). They include a delicate array of biscuits, scones, muffins, dumplings, doughnuts, pancakes, and fruit loaves. Except for the fruit loaves that require aging, quick breads are best served hot. Most quick breads freeze well and can be wrapped in foil and easily reheated to serve.

There is something special about hot biscuits or scones served with butter and jam. Tea breads spread with butter or creamed cheese make welcome additions to lunch boxes. What better way to start the day than with spicy muffins, fresh from the oven.

Here you will find a varied selection of all these and more.

Note: A statue of Sir Francis Drake holding a potato plant once stood in Offenburg, West Germany. It was erected in 1853 to honor the man credited with bringing the potato to Europe. Around the statue's base were garlands of potato leaves and inscriptions of thanks. The statue was destroyed in 1939.

POTATO BANNOCK

Bannock is the Gaelic word for cake. It is also called "Cake Bread." There are over 100 kinds of bannock. An old superstition says, "If you eat bannock on Halloween your dreams will foretell your future."

2⅓ cups all-purpose flour
1 tsp. salt
2 tbsp. baking powder
4 tbsp. sugar
2 tbsp. shortening or lard
¾ cup mashed potato
1 cup cold potato water or water

Preheat oven to 450 degrees. Sift flour, salt, baking powder, and sugar. Cut in shortening until mixture resembles coarse meal. Stir in potato. Add cold water and mix with a fork. Knead gently 8 to 10 times on a lightly floured board. Use extra flour if necessary. Pat into an oval shape about ¾ inch" thick. Score with a sharp knife. Bake for 20 minutes or until bannock sounds hollow when tapped. Serve with butter, and jam or molasses. Serves 8.

"Every country seems to top its French fries differently. The French serve them crisp and brown with salt and pepper; the Dutch and Belgians in small paper cones with a dollop of mustard and mayonnaise; the English serve fries with vinegar; the Spanish with pepper only; and all of North America love to pour on the ketchup."
-*U.S. Potato Board*

SWEET BISCUITS

These biscuits that use equal amounts of mashed potato and all-purpose flour are my husband's favorite. They can be served plain or made with a large cookie cutter and used for strawberry shortcake.

> **2 cups all-purpose flour**
> **4 tsp. baking powder**
> **¾ tsp. salt**
> **¼ cup granulated sugar**
> **½ cup shortening or margarine**
> **2 cups mashed potato**
> **⅔ cup milk, approximately (depending on the wetness of the potatoes)**

Preheat oven to 400 degrees. Combine flour, baking powder, salt, and sugar. Cut in shortening. Stir in potato and mix thoroughly. Add enough milk to make a soft dough. Knead lightly on a floured board. Cut with a biscuit cutter. Bake on a greased cookie sheet for 15 minutes. Serve hot. Makes 24 biscuits.

POTATO BISCUITS

These biscuits are quick to make and bake in only 15 minutes.

> **1½ cups all-purpose flour**
> **1 tbsp. baking powder**
> **1 tsp. salt**
> **2 tbsp. shortening**
> **½ cup cold mashed potato**
> **½ cup cold milk**

Preheat oven to 400 degrees. Combine flour, baking powder, and salt. Cut in shortening. Add potato and mix thoroughly. Add enough milk to make a soft dough. Roll lightly to ½" thickness. Cut with biscuit cutter. Bake 12 to 15 minutes. Serve hot. Makes 12 biscuits.

DUTCH BISCUITS

Of the many recipes for potato biscuits I tested while researching this book, Dutch Biscuits were unanimously voted Number One.

3 cups all-purpose flour
1 cup brown sugar
1 tsp. salt
2 tsp. cinnamon
1 tsp. baking soda
3 tsp. baking powder
¾ cup shortening
2 cups mashed potato
1 cup raisins
1 egg, slightly beaten
1 cup sour milk

Preheat oven to 425 degrees. Combine flour, brown sugar, salt, cinnamon, baking soda, and baking powder. Cut in shortening with a pastry blender until mixture resembles coarse meal. Add mashed potato and raisins. Toss lightly until potato is well-mixed into dry ingredients. Combine slightly beaten egg and sour milk. Add to other ingredients, mixing lightly with a fork. Pat to 1" thickness. Cut with a biscuit cutter. Place on greased cookie sheet. Lightly brush tops with milk if a shiny top is desired. Bake 15 to 18 minutes. Makes 24 biscuits.

Note: As part of a diet study done by New Jersey's Dr. Oscar Kruesi some years ago, 23 men were given 10 potatoes per day, which they could have prepared in any form except French fries or potato chips. "After 3 months of eating 10 potatoes a day, the average man had lost weight. Potatoes do not make a person obese . . . it is foods containing sugar and white flour [that do]. In the United States, since 1900, potato consumption has gone down 60 percent. Fats and oils have risen 50 percent. Associated with these changes has been the development of all kinds of disease . . . (Poor nutrition is often held partly responsible for heart disease, kidney ailments and diabetes.)" *-Fraser's Newsletter*

CHOCOLATE POTATO DOUGHNUTS

This recipe comes from Carol Ann Newson of Summerside, P.E.I.

2 eggs
1 cup granulated sugar
3 squares unsweetened chocolate
2 tbsp. shortening
1 cup mashed potato
3½ cups sifted all-purpose flour
6 tsp. baking powder
1 tsp. salt
¼ tsp. cinnamon
⅔ cup milk
Fat for deep frying (375 degrees)

Beat eggs until light, gradually adding sugar. Melt together unsweetened chocolate and shortening. Add potato and chocolate to first mixture. Sift dry ingredients. Fold in dry ingredients alternately with milk. Use just enough flour to make a dough that can be easily handled. Chill in refrigerator at least 1 hour. Roll to ½" thickness on a lightly floured board. Cut with a doughnut cutter. Deep fry in hot fat until brown on both sides, turning once after about 45 seconds. Drain on absorbent paper. Makes 3 dozen doughnuts.

Note: Double-Chocolate Variation: For double-chocolate doughnuts, spread slightly cooled doughnuts with a chocolate glaze.

CHOCOLATE GLAZE

1 oz. semi-sweet chocolate
2 tbsp. butter or margarine
2 tbsp. milk
1 cup icing sugar
¼ tsp. vanilla
⅛ tsp. salt

Melt chocolate. Add remaining ingredients. Blend well.

FLUFFY POTATO DOUGHNUTS

This is definitely the lightest doughnut you will ever taste.

3 eggs
1⅓ cups granulated sugar
½ tsp. vanilla
1 cup cooled mashed potato
2 tbsp. melted shortening
4 cups all-purpose flour
6 tsp. baking powder
2 tsp. nutmeg
1 tsp. salt
½ cup milk
Fat for deep frying (375 degrees)

Beat eggs with sugar and vanilla until light. Add potato and shortening and blend well. Sift together dry ingredients; add alternately with milk to potato mixture, beginning and ending with flour. Beat well. Chill 1½ hours. Heat fat for frying. While fat is heating, roll out half the dough at a time, keeping the remainder chilled. Roll to approximately ½" thickness. Cut with floured doughnut cutter. Deep fry in fat for about 3 minutes, turning once. Drain. Dip in sugar or a mixture of sugar and cinnamon. Best if served warm. Makes 3 dozen doughnuts.

"If a man really likes potatoes, he must be a decent sort of fellow . . ."
-A. A. Milne

LEMON LOAF

Light and delicious, this recipe makes a large loaf.

⅓ cup shortening
⅓ cup mashed potato
1 cup granulated sugar
2 eggs, beaten
Rind of one lemon, grated finely
1 tsp. baking powder
½ tsp. baking soda
½ tsp. salt
½ cup milk
1½ cups all-purpose flour
Juice of a half-lemon mixed with
   ⅓ cup granulated sugar (for glaze)

Preheat oven to 350 degrees. Grease a 13x4" loaf pan and line with waxed paper. Cream shortening and mashed potato. Gradually add sugar, blending well. Add eggs and lemon rind. Mix well. Sift dry ingredients and add alternately with milk, beginning and ending with dry ingredients. Mix well after each addition. Bake in prepared pan for 1 hour. Remove from oven. Spread glaze over loaf. Let stand 10 minutes. Invert on rack; remove waxed paper. Set on another cake rack in upright position to cool completely before cutting.

Note: Napoleon's army had exceptionally good dental health. Their diet consisted mainly of potatoes.

NUT LOAF

This loaf has a good old-fashioned flavor; it's rich and tender. The recipe comes from the P.E.I. Potato Marketing Board.

2 cups all-purpose flour
1 tsp. cocoa
2 tsp. baking powder
1 tsp. baking soda
¼ tsp. salt
1 cup mashed potato
½ cup milk
½ cup butter or margarine
2 cups granulated sugar
1 tsp. vanilla
1 cup finely chopped walnuts
3 egg whites

Grease and flour two 9x5" loaf pans. Preheat oven to 350 degrees. Combine flour, cocoa, baking powder, baking soda, and salt; set aside. Beat potato and milk until no lumps remain. Cream butter and sugar until light. Add vanilla. Blend in dry ingredients gradually, alternating with potato/milk mixture, beginning and ending with dry ingredients. Fold in nuts. Beat egg whites until light and fold in. Pour batter in prepared pans. Bake 30 minutes until toothpick inserted in center comes out dry.

Note: There are as many as 300 seeds in 1 potato berry. Seven hundred thousand potato seeds weigh approximately 1 pound. A small glass jar of True Potato Seed is equivalent in crop potential to 2 tons of seed potatoes.

POTATO CHERRY-NUT LOAF

The batter is a bit wetter than other loaves.

3 tbsp. butter or margarine
1 cup granulated sugar
½ cup mashed potato
2 eggs
¼ tsp. almond flavoring
2¼ cups all-purpose flour
3 tbsp. baking powder
½ tsp. salt
¼ cup maraschino cherry juice
¾ cup milk
1 cup maraschino cherries, halved
½ cup chopped walnuts

Preheat oven to 350 degrees. Grease a 13x4" loaf pan and line with waxed paper. Cream butter, sugar, and potato. Add eggs and flavoring and beat well. Combine dry ingredients. Stir cherry juice into milk. Add dry ingredients and liquids to first mixture alternately, beginning and ending with dry ingredients. Blend well. Stir in cherries and nuts. Spoon into prepared pan. Bake 1 hour or until toothpick inserted in center comes out clean.

SUGAR-GLAZED ORANGE-POTATO LOAF

The addition of mashed potato gives this loaf a lovely, moist texture.

⅓ cup shortening
1 cup granulated sugar
2 beaten eggs
1 tbsp. finely grated orange rind
Juice of 1 orange
1 tsp. baking powder
½ tsp. baking soda
¼ tsp. salt
1¾ cups all-purpose flour
½ cup mashed potato
½ cup milk
¼ cup granulated sugar

Preheat oven to 350 degrees. Grease a 9x5" loaf pan and line with waxed paper. Combine shortening, sugar, eggs, orange rind, and half the orange juice. Beat with an electric mixer until well-blended. In another bowl mix baking powder, baking soda, salt, flour, and potato. Toss lightly to evenly distribute potato through the dry ingredients. Make a well in center of dry ingredients and add shortening mixture and milk. Mix until blended. Bake 1 hour. Remove from oven. Combine remaining orange juice and ¼ cup granulated sugar. Spread over loaf. Let stand a few minutes. Remove loaf from pan, remove waxed paper, and set loaf in an upright position to cool.

POTATO FRUIT-AND-NUT BREAD

¼ cup melted butter or margarine
1 cup granulated sugar
2 well-beaten eggs
1 tbsp. finely grated orange rind
1 cup slightly warmed mashed potato
2 cups all-purpose flour
3 tsp. baking powder
1 tsp. baking soda
½ tsp. salt
1 cup raisins
¾ cup chopped walnuts
½ cup milk

Preheat oven to 350 degrees. Grease a 9x5" loaf pan and line with waxed paper. Combine butter and sugar and blend well. Add beaten eggs, orange rind, and potato. Blend thoroughly. Sift dry ingredients and mix with raisins and nuts. Add to butter-and-egg mixture alternately with milk. Blend well. Bake 1 hour or until toothpick inserted in center comes out clean.

Note: One of the newer "potato items" to be found is the potato clock. Invented by Bill Borst of Elon College in North Carolina, it is made to run on two potatoes. Copper and zinc probes are inserted in the potato and are said to cause enough flow of electrons to power the clock. The one in my office will run for 10 to 12 weeks without changing potatoes. Incidentally, it keeps perfect time.

THE POTATO COOKBOOK

POTATO-BRAN BREAD

High in iron and fiber, you can serve this bread with vegetable dishes or in lunch boxes. This recipe makes a large loaf.

1 cup bran
½ cup whole wheat flour
¾ cup all-purpose flour
1 tbsp. baking powder
½ tsp. baking soda
1 tsp. salt
⅓ cup granulated sugar
½ cup raisins
1 egg, well-beaten
¼ cup molasses
1 cup milk
¾ cup potato, cooked and mashed well

Preheat oven to 375 degrees. Grease a 9x5" loaf pan. Mix dry ingredients and raisins. Combine liquids and potato and beat with electric mixer until lumps are gone. Add dry ingredients to liquid and mix together. Fill loaf pan ⅔ full. Bake 1 hour. Allow to cool before cutting.

CORNMEAL MUFFINS

1 cup cornmeal
1 cup sour milk
½ cup all-purpose flour
¼ cup granulated sugar
½ tsp. baking soda
2 tsp. baking powder
½ cup mashed potato
1 egg, beaten
3 tbsp. vegetable oil

Mix together cornmeal and sour milk. Set aside for 10 minutes. Preheat oven to 400 degrees. Combine flour, sugar, baking soda, and baking powder. Add mashed potato to cornmeal mixture. Mix in egg and oil and beat with an electric mixer until smooth. Make a well in center of dry ingredients and add cornmeal mixture all at once. Stir quickly until ingredients are just mixed and batter is lumpy in appearance. Fill greased muffin tins ⅔ full and bake 15 to 20 minutes. Makes 12 muffins.

APPLESAUCE-DATE MUFFINS

This light tasty muffin is good for breakfast or snacks.

> ½ cup butter or margarine
> 1 cup firmly packed brown sugar
> 1 egg
> 1½ cups all-purpose flour
> 1 tsp. baking powder
> 1 tsp. baking soda
> ½ tsp. salt
> ½ tsp. cinnamon
> ½ cup finely chopped dates
> ½ cup riced potato
> ¾ cup unsweetened applesauce

Preheat oven to 375 degrees. Grease or line muffin tins. Cream together butter and brown sugar; beat in egg. Sift dry ingredients. Combine dates and potato with flour mixture. Stir into batter alternately with applesauce. Mix just until blended. Fill muffin tins ⅔ full. Bake 20 minutes. Makes 12 large muffins.

DATE-NUT MUFFINS

This recipe uses the water drained from cooking potatoes to make a fine-textured light muffin.

1 cup chopped dates
1 cup boiling potato water
3 tbsp. butter or margarine
1 cup brown sugar
1 egg, well beaten
1 tsp. vanilla
½ cup chopped walnuts
1¾ cups all-purpose flour
1 tsp. baking soda
¼ tsp. salt

Preheat oven to 350 degrees. Grease or line muffin tins. Combine dates, potato water, and butter and let cool. Blend in sugar, egg, vanilla, and nuts. Sift flour, baking soda, and salt and stir into batter. Fill greased muffin tins ⅔ full. Bake 20 to 25 minutes. Makes 18 muffins.

Note: The "potato" in other languages:

Arabic	*batata*
Dutch	*aardappel*
French	*pomme de terre*
German	*kartoffel*
Irish	*potato, pratie*
Italian	*patata*
Norwegian	*kartoffel*
Portuguese	*batata*
Spanish	*papa, patata*
Swedish	*potatis*
Swiss	*härdopfel*

BEST-EVER BLUEBERRY MUFFINS

These muffins are so moist and flavorful, buttering them isn't necessary.

1 cup buttermilk
¼ cup vegetable oil
¾ cup granulated sugar
2 eggs, beaten
2 cups all-purpose flour
1½ tsp. baking powder
1½ tsp. baking soda
⅛ tsp. nutmeg
½ tsp. salt
1 cup mashed potato
1 cup fresh blueberries

Preheat oven to 400 degrees. Grease or line muffin tins. Combine buttermilk, oil, sugar, and eggs. Mix well. Sift flour, baking powder, baking soda, nutmeg, and salt. Toss blueberries and mashed potatoes in flour mixture. Stir lightly into other ingredients. Mix only until blended. Pour into greased muffin tins, filling ¾ full. Bake 15 to 20 minutes. Makes 18 muffins.

OLD-FASHIONED ENGLISH-POTATO MUFFINS

These are quick to make on a griddle.

1 cup all-purpose flour
4 tsp. baking powder
½ tsp. salt
1 tbsp. granulated sugar
⅛ tsp. nutmeg
2 tbsp. shortening
½ cup cold mashed potato
⅓ cup milk (approximate)

THE POTATO COOKBOOK

Sift together in a mixing bowl flour, baking powder, salt, sugar, and nutmeg. Cut in shortening until the mixture resembles a coarse meal. Mash cold potato until smooth. Stir into flour mixture. Make a well in center and add milk. Mix lightly with a fork, adding a bit more milk if necessary to make a soft dough. Turn onto a lightly floured board and knead until smooth. Pat or roll to ½" thickness or less. Cut with a 3" cookie cutter. Dust a griddle with flour and heat until flour browns slightly. Bake muffins on moderately hot griddle until cooked through and golden brown, turning once (12 to 15 minutes). Serve hot with butter, honey, or jam. Makes about 12 muffins.

OATMEAL-POTATO MUFFINS

1 cup quick-cooking rolled oats
1 cup buttermilk
¾ cup cold mashed potato
½ cup brown sugar
1 egg
½ cup vegetable oil
1 tsp. vanilla
1 cup all-purpose flour
1 tsp. baking powder
½ tsp. baking soda
½ tsp. cinnamon
½ tsp. nutmeg
½ tsp. salt
1 cup raisins

Grease or line muffin tins. Combine rolled oats and buttermilk and let stand 1 hour. Preheat oven to 400 degrees. Add potato, sugar, egg, vegetable oil, and vanilla. Blend well. Sift flour, baking powder, baking soda, cinnamon, nutmeg, and salt; add raisins. Gradually add to other mixture, stirring only until blended. Pour into muffin tins. Bake 15 to 20 minutes. Makes 18 muffins.

POTATO-APPLE MUFFINS

These spicy light muffins are sure to be a favorite. Try the Blueberry-Orange variation.

½ cup raw potato, finely grated
1 cup apple, peeled and coarsely grated
⅔ cup whole wheat flour
1 cup all-purpose flour
¾ cup rolled oats
1 tbsp. baking powder
½ tsp. salt
¼ tsp. nutmeg
¾ tsp. cinnamon
1 cup brown sugar
1 egg, slightly beaten
¼ cup vegetable oil
1 cup milk

Grate potato and apple. Do not drain. Preheat oven to 400 degrees. Grease muffin tins. Measure flours, oatmeal, baking powder, salt, nutmeg, cinnamon, and brown sugar into large mixing bowl; blend. Beat together egg, oil, and milk. Add grated potato and apple. Stir into dry ingredients until mixture is thoroughly moistened. Do not overmix. Fill muffin tins ¾ full and bake 15 to 20 minutes. Makes 18 muffins.

Note: Blueberry-Orange Muffin Variation: Decrease cinnamon to ½ teaspoon. Omit grated apple. Add grated rind of 1 orange and 1 cup fresh or frozen blueberries along with the dry ingredients. Mix and bake in similar manner to above recipe.

POTATO PINEAPPLE-AND-CARROT MUFFINS

Light and delicious, hot or cold, these muffins are great for school lunch boxes.

1½ cups all-purpose flour
1 cup granulated sugar
2 tsp. baking powder
1 tsp. cinnamon
1 tsp. baking soda
1 tsp. salt
½ cup vegetable oil
2 eggs, lightly beaten
¾ cup finely grated carrot
¾ cup finely grated potato
¾ cup crushed pineapple (drain off about half the juice)

Preheat oven to 350 degrees. Lightly grease muffin tins. Combine flour, sugar, baking powder, cinnamon, baking soda, and salt in large mixing bowl. Make a well in the center of the mixture and add remaining ingredients. Mix lightly with a fork until just blended. Fill muffin tins ⅔ full. Bake 20 to 25 minutes. Makes 24 muffins.

CINNAMON-POTATO PINWHEELS

2 cups all-purpose flour
½ tsp. salt
4 tsp. baking powder
3 tbsp. shortening
1 cup mashed potato
1 cup milk
1 tsp. soft butter or margarine
¼ cup firmly packed brown sugar
1 tsp. cinnamon

Preheat oven to 400 degrees. Combine flour, salt, and baking powder. Cut in shortening until mixture resembles coarse meal. Add potato. Mix with milk to form a soft dough. Knead lightly. Roll to a 14x10" rectangle. Spread with soft butter. Mix brown sugar and cinnamon and spread over butter. Roll as a jelly roll. Seal edges. Slice in ½" slices and bake on a greased cookie sheet 12 to 15 minutes. Makes 24 pinwheels.

SPUDS'N'SPICE MUFFINS

1½ cups very finely grated raw potato
2 tsp. baking soda
1 cup whole wheat flour
½ cup all-purpose flour
3 tsp. baking powder
½ tsp. salt
¼ tsp. nutmeg
¼ tsp. ginger
¼ tsp. mace
¾ cup brown sugar
⅓ cup currants
⅓ cup raisins
⅓ cup chopped walnuts
1 egg, slightly beaten
½ cup buttermilk
⅓ cup vegetable oil
½ tsp. vanilla

Preheat oven to 400 degrees. Grease or line muffin cups. Grate potato into a large bowl, add soda, and let stand until other ingredients are assembled. Measure and sift flours, baking powder, salt, nutmeg, ginger, and mace. Add brown sugar, fruits, and nuts. Combine buttermilk, egg, oil, and vanilla. Beat well and stir into potato-soda mixture. Gradually add dry ingredients, mixing lightly just until blended. Fill muffin cups ⅔ full. Bake 20 minutes. Makes 24 muffins.

CHEESE-POTATO SCONES

These delicious cheese-topped scones come to us from Scotland.

> ⅓ cup shortening
> 1 cup hot mashed potato
> 1½ cups all-purpose flour
> ½ tsp. salt
> 4 tsp. baking powder
> ½ cup milk
> 1 egg, beaten
> ½ cup grated cheddar cheese

Preheat oven to 425 degrees. Melt shortening into hot mashed potato. Sift flour, salt, and baking powder over potato mixture. Pour in milk, all at once. Mix just enough to moisten. Turn dough out onto a lightly floured board and knead 15 times. Roll out to ½" thickness and cut into triangles. Brush tops with beaten egg. Sprinkle with finely grated cheese. Bake on a lightly greased cookie sheet for 15 to 20 minutes. Makes 18 scones.

ENGLISH POTATO TEA SCONES

This recipe, served with strawberry jam, is a favorite for Sunday tea. It is an adaptation from the kitchen of Esmé Bromley of Derbyshire, England.

> 2 cups all-purpose flour
> 4 tsp. baking powder
> ½ tsp. salt
> ¼ cup granulated sugar
> ⅛ tsp. nutmeg
> ½ cup margarine
> ¾ cup mashed potato
> ¾ cup raisins or currants
> 1 egg mixed with enough milk to make ⅔ cup

Preheat oven to 400 degrees. Combine dry ingredients. Cut in margarine. Thoroughly combine until mixture is crumbly. Add mashed potato and fruit. Toss lightly. Gently stir in egg-and-milk mixture using a fork. Mix only until blended. Knead lightly 3 or 4 times. Pat to 1" thickness. Cut with a biscuit cutter or knife. Bake on a greased cookie sheet for 15 minutes. Makes 24 scones.

Note: For a shiny golden top, I like to brush a bit of milk over the scones before baking.

CURRANT-POTATO SCONES

These are quick to make, simple, and delicious.

1¾ cups all-purpose flour
¼ cup granulated sugar
1 tbsp. baking powder
1 tsp. salt
⅓ cup butter, shortening, or margarine
¾ cup mashed potato
¼ cup currants
⅓ cup milk
1 whole egg
1 egg yolk
1 egg white
Granulated sugar

Preheat oven to 425 degrees. Combine flour, sugar, baking powder, and salt. Cut in butter until mixture resembles coarse meal. Add potato. Mix lightly. Stir in currants. Mix together milk, whole egg, and egg yolk. Stir with fork into dry ingredients until well-moistened. Turn dough onto a lightly floured board. Knead gently about 20 strokes. Roll into a circle with dough ½" thick. Brush with slightly beaten egg white and sprinkle with sugar. Cut in 12 pie-shaped wedges and place on greased baking sheet. Bake 12 to 15 minutes. Makes 12 scones.

YEAST BREADS

It is said that every cook since Cleopatra has at some time wanted to bake bread. No other culinary skill gives such personal satisfaction as the thrill of just-baked bread.

The early Egyptians were the first to discover a form of yeast. Since then, bread-making has had an important role in history. At one time the Greeks allowed only priests to make bread. The Romans turned bread-making over to the Civil Service. Bread has long been one of our most important and economical foods—as part of our heritage it is aptly called the "staff of life." Adding potatoes to bread dough makes for a moister loaf that keeps longer.

Bread-making is no longer the arduous all-day task our grandmothers knew. Today, quick-rising yeast and bread-kneading appliances have made bread-making a simple task.

The recipes here are written to be easily understood and followed to perfect results, even if you have never baked bread before. Read the recipes carefully and follow the basic rules and you will have beautiful bread every time.

Hints for Making Better Bread

The water used to dissolve yeast should be about 105 degrees. To test the temperature, put a drop of water on the inside of your wrist. It should feel warm, but not hot. Water that is too hot will kill yeast action.

With the first addition of flour, beat the batter well to ensure that all ingredients are blended.

To knead dough, fold toward you and then push away with the heel of your hand. Rotate dough a quarter-turn and repeat until dough is smooth and surface looks blistered. A good way to tell if dough has been kneaded enough is to pinch the dough with one hand and at the same time squeeze your ear lobe. They will feel about the same.

Cover dough and set to rise in a warm, draft-free place.

To test for doubled bulk, stick fingertips into dough; the marks should remain if dough is doubled. To punch down, shut your fist and plunge it into the center of the dough.

Bake breads with the top of the pan level with the middle of the oven. Be sure pans have space all the way around them and are not touching the sides of the oven. Bread is done when you tap the crust and it sounds hollow. Remove bread from pans and place on wire racks to cool. Cool away from drafts.

Store bread in a tightly covered breadbox at room temperature, or wrap in foil or plastic wrap and put in your freezer. Bread dries out quickly if kept in the refrigerator.

POTATO BREAD

This is an economical bread that's extra special toasted and freezes well.

1 cup lukewarm potato water
2 tsp. sugar
2 tbsp. yeast
2 cups scalded milk
1 cup mashed potato
2 tbsp. sugar
2½ tsp. salt
3 tbsp. vegetable oil
8 to 8½ cups all-purpose flour

Combine potato water and sugar, stir well until sugar dissolves. Sprinkle with yeast and let stand 10 minutes. Meanwhile, scald milk and mix with mashed potato, sugar, salt, and oil. Cool to lukewarm and add to yeast mixture. Add about half the flour and beat until smooth. Gradually mix the remaining flour to make a stiff dough. Turn onto a floured board and knead until smooth, about 8 minutes. Add extra flour if necessary. Place dough in a lightly greased bowl, turning the dough over to grease both sides. Cover with a towel and let rise until double in bulk. Punch down and turn onto a lightly floured board. Divide into 4 equal portions, cover and let rest for 10 to 15 minutes. Shape into 4 loaves and place in greased 8x4" loaf pans. Cover and let rise until doubled, about 1 hour. Bake in preheated oven at 350 degrees for 30 to 35 minutes. Cool on wire racks. Makes 4 loaves.

Note: The title of the world's oldest potato cookbook, written in 1664, is *England's Happiness Increased . . . or a Sure and Easie Remedy against all succeeding Dear Years by A Plantation of the Roots called POTATOES, whereof (with the Addition of Wheat flour) excellent food and wholesome Bread may be made, every Year, eight or nine months together, for half the Charge as formerly. ALSO by the planting of these ROOTS, Ten thousand Men in England and Wales, who know not how to Live, or what to get Maintenance for their Families, may of One Acre of Ground, make Thirty Pounds per Annum, Invented and Published for the Good of the Poorer Sort by John Forster, Gent.*

POTATO DOUGH WITH VARIATIONS

This great recipe will yield 100 rolls or doughnuts. It was given to me by Sue Carson of Indiana, U.S.

3 tbsp. dry yeast
1 tsp. granulated sugar
1 cup lukewarm water
4 cups scalded milk
2 cups mashed potato
1 cup margarine or butter
1 cup granulated sugar
18 cups all-purpose flour, divided
2 beaten eggs
1 tbsp. salt

Dissolve 1 tsp. sugar in lukewarm water. Sprinkle yeast over top and let sit for 10 minutes. Combine scalded milk, potato, margarine, and sugar. Cool to lukewarm. Add yeast mixture and 6 cups flour. Mix well. Let stand until mixture foams (about 20 minutes). Add beaten eggs, salt, and enough flour to make a stiff dough. Knead well. Put in a greased bowl and let rise until double in bulk. Punch down. Divide dough into 4 equal portions.

DOUGHNUTS

Roll out to ¾" thickness. Cut with doughnut cutter. Place on trays and let rise until not quite doubled. Fry in hot oil (375 degrees). Drain on brown paper. Glaze while hot with the following mixture:

1 lb. icing sugar
1 tbsp. margarine
1 tsp. vanilla
dash of mace
2 to 3 tbsp. milk (to make a thin glaze)

Combine all ingredients and mix well.

CINNAMON BUNS

Roll dough into a rectangle, about 18x9". Spread with butter. Sprinkle with a mixture of brown sugar and cinnamon. Roll like a jelly roll. Cut in 1½" slices. Place on greased pans. Cover and let rise until nearly doubled. Bake in a preheated oven at 400 degrees for 15 to 20 minutes. Glaze with doughnut glaze.

STICKY BUNS

Handle dough as for cinnamon buns. Grease pans heavily. Put a mixture of brown sugar, butter, corn syrup, and cinnamon in bottom of pans. Put rolls on top. Let rise and bake as for cinnamon buns. Invert pan as soon as it is removed from the oven.

DINNER ROLLS

Shape dough in desired ways. Place on greased pans. Let rise until nearly doubled. Bake in preheated oven at 400 degrees for 15 minutes. Brush tops with melted butter.

COFFEE CAKE

Put any scraps of remaining dough in a greased pan. Punch holes in dough with a spoon handle. Spread any leftover sugar, butter, syrup, and cinnamon on top. Bake as for cinnamon buns. Use any leftover glaze to put on hot coffee cake.

All of these freeze well. Simply let cool and wrap in plastic.

Note: Several studies have shown that children consistently choose potatoes when asked to name their favorite vegetable.

FLUFFY POTATO ROLLS

1 tbsp. dry yeast
¼ cup lukewarm water
½ cup hot mashed potato
¼ cup shortening
¼ cup sugar
1½ tsp. salt
1 cup scalded milk
1 egg
4 to 4½ cups all purpose flour

Dissolve yeast in warm water. Combine potato, shortening, sugar, salt, and hot milk. Cool to lukewarm. Add dissolved yeast and egg. Stir in flour to make a soft dough. Knead lightly on a floured surface until smooth and elastic (6 to 8 minutes). Place in a lightly greased bowl, turning over once to grease both sides. Cover. Let rise until double in bulk (about 1 hour). Punch down. Shape into a ball. Cover and let rest for 10 minutes. Shape into rolls. Place on a greased cookie sheet. Cover loosely and let rise until almost double in bulk (about 1 hour). Bake in a preheated 400-degree oven for 10 to 12 minutes. Makes 2 dozen rolls.

"Always buy the best
Our spuds have good taste
And served properly
Won't go to your waist." -*Sign in a potato display at a grocery store*

SOUTHERN POTATO BREAD

1 medium potato
¼ cup vegetable oil
¼ cup granulated sugar
1 tsp. salt
1 tsp. granulated sugar
1 tbsp. dry yeast
¼ cup lukewarm water
1 egg
⅓ cup milk
3 to 3½ cups all-purpose flour
Vegetable oil
Melted butter

Peel potato, cut in chunks, and boil until soft. Reserve water. Mash potato and add ½ cup potato water. Stir in vegetable oil, ¼ cup sugar, and salt; mix well. Add remaining 1 tsp. sugar and yeast to lukewarm water. Stir until dissolved. Set for 5 minutes until foamy. Add to potato mixture. Beat egg lightly and combine with milk. Add to potato mixture. In a large bowl, combine potato mixture and flour. Blend well to make a soft dough. Turn out on floured board and knead until smooth and elastic, about 10 minutes, using additional flour if necessary. Place in a greased bowl and turn dough over so both sides are greased. Cover tightly with plastic wrap and set in a warm place to rise until double in bulk. Punch down and knead lightly. Shape into a loaf and place in a greased 9x5" pan. Brush top with vegetable oil. Cover with plastic wrap and let rise until double in bulk. Preheat oven to 400 degrees. Bake loaf for 25 to 35 minutes until it sounds hollow when tapped. Turn out on wire rack to cool. Brush top with melted butter. Do not slice until completely cool. Makes 1 loaf.

"The man who has not anything to boast of but his illustrious ancestors is like the potato—the only good thing belonging to him is underground." -Sir Thomas Overbury, 1613

POTATO PARKERHOUSE ROLLS

Folding circles of dough in half makes the Parkerhouse shape.

1 tbsp. yeast
1 tsp. granulated sugar
½ cup lukewarm water
1 cup mashed potato
7 cups all-purpose flour, divided
¾ cup shortening
½ cup granulated sugar
2 tsp. salt
2 well-beaten eggs
1 cup scalded milk, cooled to lukewarm

Dissolve yeast and sugar in lukewarm water. Set aside for 10 minutes. Combine potato, 1 cup flour, shortening, sugar, and salt. Add eggs and milk. Stir in yeast mixture. Cover and set in a warm place to rise for 2 hours. Add 6 cups of flour and knead well. Cover and let rise until double in bulk, about 1½ hours. Roll to ¼" thickness; cut with 2½" cookie cutter. Fold each roll over to form Parkerhouse shape. Let rise on a greased cookie sheet until double in bulk, about 1½ hours. Preheat oven to 425 degrees. Bake 30 to 35 minutes. Makes 30 rolls.

"To me they are glamorous, unique and special, an aristocrat among vegetables."
-James Beard, the famous chef, on potatoes

POTATO REFRIGERATOR ROLLS

The dough for this recipe can be prepared and stored for several days in the refrigerator before using.

1 cup warm mashed potato
1½ cups warm potato water or water
1 tbsp. dry yeast
⅔ cup granulated sugar
1½ tsp. salt
⅔ cup soft shortening
2 eggs, slightly beaten
7 to 7½ cups all-purpose flour

Cook potatoes; drain, reserving 1½ cups potato water. Dissolve yeast in potato water. Let stand 10 minutes. Add sugar, salt, shortening, eggs, and mashed potato. Mix well. Add flour gradually and mix until smooth and elastic. Place in a greased bowl and turn over to grease the other side. Cover with a damp cloth and place in the refrigerator for at least 2 hours. Remove the desired amount of dough and shape into rolls. Cover and let rise until doubled, about 1½ to 2 hours. Bake for about 10 to 12 minutes in preheated 400-degree oven. Makes 4 dozen rolls.

"There is no species of human food that can be consumed in greater variety of modes than the potato." -*Sir John Sinclair, 1828*

ACADIAN BUNS

An eighteenth-century recipe, these buns are excellent for twentieth-century hamburgers.

> **2 cups water**
> **2 medium potatoes**
> **1 tbsp. yeast**
> **2 tsp. sugar**
> **½ cup water**
> **7 to 7½ cups all-purpose flour**
> **¾ cup lard***
> **2½ tsp. salt**
> **1 egg**
> **2 tbsp. sugar**

Boil potatoes in water. Drain off ½ cup potato water. Set aside. Mash potatoes in remaining water. Let cool to lukewarm. Dissolve 2 tsp. sugar in the ½ cup water and ½ cup reserved potato water (cooled to lukewarm). Sprinkle with 1 tbsp. yeast. Let stand 10 minutes. Blend 6 cups flour, lard, and salt. Beat egg and 2 tbsp. sugar; add to yeast mixture. Gradually add dry ingredients. Mix well. Turn onto lightly floured board and knead until dough does not stick to hands, using extra flour if necessary. Let rise 1½ to 2 hours, until very light. Form into 36 buns. Place on 3 lightly greased cookie sheets, leaving space for spreading. Let rise until double in bulk, about 45 minutes. Bake in a preheated 400-degree oven for 15 to 18 minutes. Makes 36 buns.

*Be sure to use lard and *not* shortening in this recipe.

Note: Even though some foods contain higher individual amounts of Vitamin C, potatoes, because of their greater popularity and consumption, rank second only to the total of all citrus fruits in the amount of Vitamin C contributed.

Canada's Food Guide recommends one serving of potato each day.

CHELSEA BUNS

A family favorite, these "sticky buns" are made as a special treat for birthday breakfasts.

½ cup lukewarm potato water
½ cup cooled mashed potato
1 tsp. sugar
1 tbsp. dry yeast
¼ cup butter or margarine, melted
¼ cup granulated sugar
2 eggs, well-beaten
½ tsp. salt
3 cups all-purpose flour (approximate)
2 tbsp. soft butter or margarine
¼ cup corn syrup
½ cup brown sugar
¼ tsp. vanilla
½ cup coarsely chopped walnuts
2 tbsp. soft butter or margarine
½ cup brown sugar
1½ tsp. cinnamon
½ cup raisins

Combine potato water, mashed potato, sugar, and yeast. Let stand in a warm place for 10 minutes. Add melted butter, granulated sugar, and eggs. Beat well. Add salt and enough flour to make a soft dough. Knead on a lightly floured board until smooth and elastic. Place in a greased bowl. Turn over to lightly grease top of dough. Cover and let rise until double in bulk, about 1½ hours. Grease two 8" cake pans. Spread bottom of pans with mixture of soft butter, corn syrup, brown sugar, vanilla, and walnuts. Roll dough into a 10x20" rectangle. Spread with soft butter and sprinkle with brown sugar, cinnamon, and raisins. Roll as for jelly roll and cut into 32 even pieces. Place in pan. Cover and let rise about 1 hour. Bake in a preheated oven at 375 degrees for 10 minutes. Reduce heat to 350 degrees and bake another 15 to 20 minutes. Cool a few minutes and invert pan on waxed paper or a plate. Makes 32 buns.

EASY HOT CROSS BUNS

The flavors of nutmeg and citron make these old favorites just a bit different.

½ cup hot mashed potato
½ cup scalded milk
½ cup boiling potato water
⅓ cup margarine
⅓ cup granulated sugar
1 tsp. salt
1 tsp. finely grated orange rind
½ cup lukewarm water, or potato water
1 tsp. granulated sugar
2 tbsp. dry yeast
2 tsp. cinnamon
½ tsp. nutmeg
¼ tsp. cloves
½ cup currants
½ cup raisins
½ cup citron peel
4 to 5 cups all-purpose flour
2 well-beaten eggs

Combine potato, milk, potato water, margarine, sugar, salt, and orange rind. Stir until margarine melts. Cool to lukewarm. Meanwhile, dissolve 1 tsp. sugar in lukewarm water. Sprinkle yeast over the top and let stand for 10 minutes. Combine spices, fruits, and 2 cups flour. Beat into potato mixture. Add yeast and eggs. Blend well. Stir in enough additional flour to make a stiff dough. Knead well. Let rise until double in bulk, about 1½ hours. Form into 24 flat buns. Cut a cross on top of each bun with a sharp knife. Place on greased cookie sheets. Let rise until doubled. Bake in a preheated oven at 400 degrees for 15 to 18 minutes. Glaze while hot with doughnut glaze (see Doughnuts) if desired. Makes 24 buns.

BAGELS

1 medium potato
2½ cups water
1 tbsp. dry yeast
1½ tsp. honey
1 tbsp. vegetable oil
1 tbsp. honey
1 whole egg
1 egg white (reserve yolk for glaze)
5 cups all-purpose flour (approximate)
3 qts water

GLAZE

1 egg yolk
1 tsp. cold water
Poppy or sesame seeds

Boil sliced potato in 2½ cups water until soft. Drain, reserving water. Mash potato. Cool water to lukewarm. Start yeast in ½ cup potato water and 1½ tsp. honey. To remaining potato water add oil, 1 tbsp. honey, yeast mixture, mashed potato, egg, egg white, and flour. When dough is stiff, knead for 8 to 10 minutes, adding extra flour if necessary. Place dough in a greased pan. Cover and let rise until almost double in bulk, about 45 minutes. Punch down and let rise again for 45 minutes. Shape dough into three 12" rolls. Cut each one into 8 equal pieces. Form each piece into a small roll. Moisten ends and form bagels. Let rise about 15 minutes. Meanwhile heat the 3 quarts of water to boiling. Reduce heat and simmer the bagels (a few at a time) for 5 minutes, turning once. Drain and place on lightly oiled cookie sheets. Preheat oven to 425 degrees. Brush bagels with the glaze mixture and sprinkle with poppy or sesame seeds. Bake for 15 to 20 minutes. Cool on a wire rack. Makes 24 bagels.

SUGAR & SPICE LOAF

This recipe makes 6 loaves of deliciously spicy bread. It is easy to make half the recipe; however, since Sugar & Spice Loaf freezes so well I always make the full amount.

1 cup mashed potato
2 cups boiling potato water or water
2½ cups milk, scalded
½ cup molasses
½ cup brown sugar
1 cup lard or shortening
3 tbsp. dry yeast
3 tsp. granulated sugar
½ cup lukewarm water
2 beaten eggs
6 cups whole wheat flour
3 tsp. salt
3 tsp. cinnamon
1 tsp. nutmeg
1 tsp. ginger
½ tsp. cloves
2 cups raisins
6 to 8 cups all-purpose flour

Combine potato, boiling water, milk, molasses, brown sugar, and lard. Mix well. Cool to lukewarm. Meanwhile, dissolve yeast and granulated sugar in lukewarm water. Let stand 10 minutes. Combine potato mixture and yeast. Add eggs, whole wheat flour, salt, spices, and raisins. Beat well. Mix in enough all-purpose flour to make a stiff dough. Knead on a lightly floured board for 8 to 10 minutes, adding flour as needed to prevent sticking. Cover and let rise in a greased bowl for about 1½ hours. Shape into 6 loaves. Place in 8x4" greased loaf pans. Let rise 45 minutes. Bake in a preheated oven at 350 degrees for 50 minutes. Makes 6 loaves.

OLD-FASHIONED PLUM LOAF

From nineteenth-century Scotland, this recipe is sure to be a hit with everyone. It also freezes well.

2 cups scalded milk
1½ cups boiling potato water, or water
1 cup mashed potato
¾ cup brown sugar
½ cup shortening
½ cup lukewarm water
2 tbsp. granulated sugar
2 tbsp. dry yeast
8 cups all-purpose flour
2 tsp. cinnamon
1 tsp. nutmeg
2 tsp. salt
1 tsp. baking soda
2 cups seeded raisins
1 to 2 cups additional all-purpose flour

While milk is scalding, combine potato water, mashed potato, brown sugar, and shortening. Add to milk. Cool to lukewarm. Meanwhile, dissolve 2 tbsp. sugar in ½ cup lukewarm water. Sprinkle yeast over the top and let stand 10 minutes. Mix flour, cinnamon, nutmeg, salt, and baking soda. Coat raisins in ¼ cup of this dry mixture. Combine yeast with potato mixture and add about half of the dry ingredients. Beat well. Stir in raisins and remaining dry ingredients to make a stiff dough. Knead 8 to 10 minutes, using additional flour if necessary. Cover and let rise 1½ hours. Form into 4 loaves. Let rise 1 hour. Bake in preheated 350-degree oven for 50 to 60 minutes. Makes 4 loaves.

Note: If using water instead of potato water, the rising time may be a few minutes longer.

SPUDNUTS

This recipe is from the kitchen of Isabel Campbell, who writes, "It has become an established habit to make a batch of 'Spudnuts' several times during the winter, for the men in the warehouse grading potatoes. They look forward to 'Spudnut Day.' Besides being delicious, it breaks up their day."

1 tbsp. dry yeast
1 tsp. granulated sugar
¼ cup lukewarm water
2 cups scalded milk
½ cup butter or margarine
¾ tsp. salt
2 well-beaten eggs
1 cup mashed potato
½ cup granulated sugar
6½ cups all-purpose flour (approximate)
Oil for deep frying

Dissolve yeast and sugar in lukewarm water. Let stand 10 minutes. Scald milk and add butter and salt. Cool to lukewarm. Add eggs and blend well. Combine mashed potato and sugar; add milk mixture along with yeast. Mix well. Add enough all-purpose flour to make a soft dough. Let double in size in a warm place (about 3½ hours). Roll to ½" thickness. Cover and let rise until doubled. Heat oil for frying to 360 degrees. Snip small squares off the dough with scissors and quickly drop into hot oil. Brown on each side. Drain on rack. While hot, dip in glaze. Makes 4 dozen.

SPUDNUT GLAZE

2 tbsp. butter or margarine
2 tbsp. hot milk
½ tsp. vanilla
2 cups icing sugar (approximate)

Combine ingredients and mix to a spreading consistency.

FASTNACHTS

Begin these special treats early in the day for a welcome homecoming to school children. Fastnachts come to us from Germany.

1 cup warm potato water
¾ cup granulated sugar
1 tsp. salt
7 to 8 cups all-purpose flour
1 tsp. granulated sugar
¼ cup lukewarm water
1 tbsp. dry yeast
1 cup hot mashed potato
½ cup soft margarine or butter
¼ tsp. nutmeg
Fat for deep frying

Combine potato water, ¾ cup sugar, salt, and 1 cup flour. Beat until smooth. Mix together 1 tsp. sugar, lukewarm water, and yeast. Stir to dissolve. Blend the two mixtures, cover and let stand in a warm place until bubbly (3 to 4 hours). Beat together hot mashed potato, margarine, and nutmeg. Stir potato mixture into yeast mixture, adding enough flour to make a fairly stiff dough. Turn out on a lightly floured board and knead until smooth and elastic. Place in a greased bowl; cover and let rise in a warm place until double in bulk (1½ hours). Punch down and store in refrigerator until ready to use. Roll out to ⅓" thickness and cut with a doughnut cutter. Place on a floured board, cover, and let rise another 1 to 1¼ hours. Heat fat to 365 degrees. Fry fastnachts (4 at a time) in hot fat. When they rise to the surface, turn them over. Fry until brown on both sides. Drain on absorbent paper. Dust with sugar. Makes 3 to 4 dozen.

Note: Prince Edward Island is known as "Spud Island." This title is earned by the production of some of the finest seed and table potatoes grown in the world.

SPICY ORANGE-POTATO DOUGHNUTS

5 to 5½ cups all-purpose flour
½ cup granulated sugar
1 tsp. salt
1 tbsp. grated orange rind
2 tbsp. instant dry yeast*
1 cup lukewarm water
¼ cup margarine or butter
½ cup mashed potato
1 egg
Oil for deep frying
1 cup granulated sugar
2 tsp. cinnamon

Mix thoroughly 1½ cups of the flour, ½ cup sugar, salt, orange rind, and yeast. Heat the water and margarine to lukewarm and gradually add to the dry ingredients. Beat 2 minutes. Add potato, egg, and ½ cup of the flour. Beat 2 minutes. Add remaining flour and stir to make a soft dough. Turn onto a lightly floured board and knead until smooth and elastic (about 8 to 10 minutes). Place in a greased bowl, turning over to grease the top. Cover and allow to rise until double in bulk, about 1 hour. Punch down, roll out to ½" thickness and cut with a 3" doughnut cutter. Place doughnuts on greased baking sheets. Cover and let rise until double in bulk, about 30 minutes. Deep fry in oil at 375 degrees until golden brown on both sides. Drain on absorbent paper. Combine the remaining sugar and cinnamon, and dip doughnuts in this mixture. Makes about 36 doughnuts.

*If using regular yeast, dissolve in ½ cup lukewarm water before adding to dry ingredients.

IRISH FRECKLE BREAD

This is a pioneer recipe with just a few big seeded raisins.

1 small potato
2 cups water
1 tsp. granulated sugar
2 tbsp. dry yeast
½ cup soft margarine or butter
½ cup granulated sugar
2 eggs, beaten
1 tsp. salt
6 cups all-purpose flour (approximate)
1 cup seeded raisins

Boil potato in water until very tender. Drain, reserving water. Mash potato, set aside. Measure ½ cup potato water into a small bowl; cool to lukewarm. Add 1 tsp. sugar; stir. Add yeast and let stand for 10 minutes. Meanwhile, combine remaining potato water, margarine, and ½ cup sugar. Stir until margarine is melted. Add beaten eggs, salt, and ¼ cup of the mashed potato. Stir in raisins and enough additional flour to make a soft dough. Knead on a lightly floured board until smooth and elastic. Place in a greased bowl. Lightly grease top of dough. Cover and let rise until double in bulk, about 1 hour. Punch down. Shape into 4 loaves. Put in greased 8" loaf pans. Cover and let rise until double in bulk, about 45 minutes. Bake in preheated oven at 350 degrees for 35 minutes. Makes 4 loaves.

Note: An American football game held annually in Monte Vista, Colorado, is called "the Spud Bowl."

GOLDEN CORN BREAD

½ cup warm water
1 tsp. sugar
1 tbsp. dry yeast
1½ cups hot potato water
1 cup warm mashed potato
1 cup cornmeal
¼ cup corn syrup
¼ cup shortening
2 tsp. salt
4 cups all-purpose flour

Combine warm water, sugar, and yeast; let stand 10 minutes. Combine potato water, mashed potato, cornmeal, corn syrup, shortening, and salt. Let stand until yeast mixture is ready. Add yeast mixture to potato mixture along with 2 cups flour. Beat well. Stir in enough additional flour to make a stiff dough. Knead on a lightly floured board, adding more flour if necessary. Let rest 15 minutes. Shape into 2 loaves. Place in greased 8x4" loaf pans. Cover and let rise until dough reaches top of pans. Bake in preheated 400-degree oven for 15 minutes, then reduce heat to 350 degrees and bake for 25 minutes. If desired, brush tops of loaves with melted butter after removing from oven. Makes 2 small loaves.

Note: One of the first planting and harvesting tools used in growing potatoes was a hoe-type instrument called a "spud." When harvesting potatoes, one would go "spudding." Many people say the nickname "spud" came from the ancient farm implement.

FROSTED FRUIT RING

Our daughter Marina was 8 years old when she adapted this recipe from a magazine. Frosted Fruit Ring, alias "Marina's Christmas Bread," has become a tradition at our house.

1¼ cups cream of potato soup* (one 10-oz. can)
¾ cup potato water
½ cup margarine or butter
3 cups all-purpose flour
2 tbsp. instant dry yeast
½ tsp. salt
3 tbsp. granulated sugar
3 eggs, well-beaten
½ cup candied mixed fruit
½ cup golden raisins
½ cup candied cherries, quartered
3 to 3½ cups all-purpose flour

Combine soup, water, and margarine in a saucepan. Heat over medium heat until margarine is melted and mixture is lukewarm. Pour into a large mixing bowl. Combine flour, yeast, salt, and sugar. Add to potato mixture. Stir in eggs and beat at medium speed for 3 to 4 minutes until well-blended. Stir in by hand fruit and enough flour to make a stiff dough. Knead on a lightly floured board, using additional flour as required until dough is smooth and satiny and does not stick to your hands. Place in a greased bowl, turning over once to grease both sides. Cover and let rise until double in bulk, about 1 hour. Roll half the dough into a 24x6" rectangle. Cut into 3 lengthwise strips. Form the strips into a braid and place in 2 greased 10" tubepans. Cover and let rise until doubled, about 1 hour. Bake in a preheated oven at 375 degrees for 20 to 25 minutes. Glaze with a confectioner's glaze if desired. Makes 2 rings.

*If potato soup is lumpy, sieve or whirl in blender.

HONEY WHOLE WHEAT BREAD

This is delicious warm from the oven with home-baked beans.

> **4 cups whole wheat flour**
> **½ cup dry milk powder**
> **2 tbsp. yeast**
> **1 tbsp. salt**
> **2½ cups potato water**
> **½ cup honey**
> **2 tbsp. oil**
> **4 cups white all-purpose flour (more if necessary)**

Dissolve 1 tsp. sugar in ½ cup warm water, and mix 3 cups whole wheat flour, dry milk powder, yeast, and salt in a large bowl. Heat the potato water, honey, and oil until warm, about 120-130 degrees. Pour over flour mixture. Beat with electric mixer 3 minutes. Stir in remaining cup of whole wheat flour and white flour. Knead 5 minutes using additional flour if necessary. Let rise in greased bowl until double in bulk, about 1½ hours. Punch down and divide in half. Form 2 loaves. Place in greased 9x5" loaf pans. Cover and let rise 40 to 45 minutes. Bake in 375-degree oven for 40 to 45 minutes. Makes 2 large loaves.

Note: Variation: Add ¼ cup wheat germ.

POTATO-WATER SOURDOUGH

No potato cookbook would be complete without a recipe for sourdough. One of the first baking products made with potatoes was potato yeast or potato sourdough. Used before the invention of baking powder, the first recipes were made with hops. Today we use regular dry yeast with equally satisfying results.

Early pioneers depended on sourdough as their main leavening agent. Today it is used as an enhancer to baked goods, giving a lighter texture and superior taste. There are many variations of sourdough starter. I have included my favorite. Sourdough can be made using raw potato, mashed potato, or simply potato water. It can be used again and again by simply measuring out the required amount for your recipe and "feeding" the remaining starter with equal amounts of all-purpose flour and lukewarm water, at least once a week. Let starter sit at room temperature for 12 hours after feeding. If a clear liquid appears on top of your starter, simply stir.

Keep a supply of sourdough starter on hand. There's no end to the possibilities for its use.

2½ cups potato water, lukewarm (be sure water is not too hot)
1¾ cups all-purpose flour
1 tbsp. salt
1 tbsp. granulated sugar
1 tbsp. dry yeast

In a medium bowl combine flour, salt, sugar, and yeast. Mix well. Stir in potato water. Cover with a towel and set in a warm place, free from drafts, for 48 hours. Mixture will become bubbly. Stir the mixture several times a day. Store in refrigerator in glass or plastic container with a hole punched in the cover. "Feed" your sourdough once a week with 1 cup flour and 1 cup lukewarm water. I remove my starter from the refrigerator the night before I want to use it. I measure out the amount I will use, feed the remainder, and leave it out overnight before returning it to the refrigerator.

Note: Thomas Jefferson is credited with having introduced French fries into the White House, sometime in 1801.

CHEESE-AND-POTATO SOURDOUGH BREAD

This makes 2 loaves of an old-country classic.

2 tbsp. dry yeast
½ cup lukewarm water
1 tsp. sugar
1 cup sourdough starter
2 cups lukewarm potato water or water
1½ cups grated cheddar cheese
½ tsp. baking powder
2 tbsp. vegetable oil
2 tbsp. granulated sugar
2 tbsp. salt
2 cups mashed potato
7 cups all-purpose flour (approximate)

Combine yeast, water, and sugar. Let stand 10 minutes. Mix remaining ingredients together (except flour). Mix well. Add dissolved yeast and gradually add flour. Stir well after each addition. Add enough flour to make a firm dough. Knead on a lightly floured surface until smooth and elastic, using additional flour if necessary. Lightly grease dough. Place in a warm bowl; cover and set in a draft-free place to rise until doubled. Punch down, form into loaves. Let rise 2 hours in greased loaf pans. Preheat oven to 375 degrees and bake 45 minutes. Makes 2 loaves.

COOKIES

The first time your children raid the cupboards, chances are they will be looking for cookies. Soon they'll want to bake them too! Milk and cookies have welcomed the new kid on the block, helped heal scraped knees, and sealed friendship pacts for children over the decades. Equally good in lunch boxes, at picnics, on a hike, or for a TV or late-night snack, cookies symbolize a friendly home.

Note: Brigitte Van Vliet of Albany, Prince Edward Island, tells how potatoes saved her and her family from starvation:

"During the last winter of World War II, food and fuel shortages caused untold suffering and death to thousands of people in the western part of Holland, where I lived at the time.

"To feed the family, my father tried very hard to supplement the meager food rations. A market gardener and fruit grower, he had never grown potatoes before; yet somehow he managed to obtain a falsified permit to grow spuds. It took him 5 days to bring the small seed potatoes home by barge. They were stored in a pit in the ground and were covered with straw and clay.

"Once a week, we took out 7 buckets of spuds, each bucket enough for 3 meals per day. As the winter progressed, however, the potatoes were disappearing too fast and the rations becoming smaller and smaller. By February, we added sugar beets and crushed tulip bulbs to our diet to stretch the potato supply.

"At the end of the war in May, we could only be thankful that our family was saved from starvation by a barge load of potatoes."

DOUBLE-CHOCOLATE POTATO COOKIES

½ cup shortening
1 cup brown sugar, firmly packed
1 egg
1 tsp. vanilla
2 squares unsweetened chocolate, melted
½ cup mashed potato (room temperature)
½ tsp. salt
½ tsp. baking soda
¾ cup sour milk
½ cup chopped nuts

Preheat oven to 400 degrees. Cream together shortening and brown sugar until light and fluffy. Beat in egg and vanilla, mixing well. Add chocolate and mashed potato and beat until smooth. Sift together flour, salt, and baking soda. Add alternately with sour milk to creamed mixture. Stir until smooth. Add nuts. Drop by rounded teaspoons on a greased baking sheet. Bake about 10 minutes or until they spring back when touched. Do not overbake. Cool slightly. Makes 40 cookies.

FROSTING

1 tbsp. soft butter or margarine
1 square unsweetened chocolate, melted
1½ tbsp. warm water
1 cup icing sugar, sifted

Combine ingredients; mix well. Spread over cookies.

"The potato is the world's greatest plant." -*W.F. Wright, 1917*

COCONUT-CRUNCH COOKIES

1 cup soft shortening
1 cup brown sugar
1 cup granulated sugar
2 eggs, slightly beaten
1 tsp. almond extract
1 tsp. vanilla
1½ cups all-purpose flour
1 tsp. baking soda
1 tsp. baking powder
¼ tsp. salt
¼ tsp. cloves
½ tsp. nutmeg
2 cups shredded coconut
1 cup crushed potato chips
2 cups rolled oats

Preheat oven to 375 degrees. Combine shortening, sugars, and eggs in a large mixing bowl. Beat until light and fluffy. Stir in almond and vanilla flavorings. Sift flour, baking soda, baking powder, salt, cloves, and nutmeg. Blend into creamed mixture. Stir in coconut, potato chips, and rolled oats. Roll in small balls. Place on a greased cookie sheet. Flatten with a fork. Bake 12 to 15 minutes. These cookies will become crisp as they cool. Makes 6 dozen.

Note: It takes 23 medium potatoes to make up 2500 calories, the daily required calories of an average adult. On top of his regular diet, a person would have to eat 11 pounds of potatoes to put on 1 pound of weight.

HOLIDAY HERMITS

This is a holiday recipe that you will want to use all year round.

1 cup soft shortening or margarine
2 cups brown sugar, firmly packed
2 large eggs
1 cup mashed potato
½ cup potato water
3 cups all-purpose flour
1 tsp. salt
1 tsp. baking soda
1 tsp. nutmeg
1 tsp. cinnamon
1 tsp. instant coffee
1 cup chopped walnuts
1 cup seedless raisins or chopped dates

Preheat oven to 400 degrees. Cream shortening and sugar. Add eggs, potato, and potato water; beat well. Sift together flour, salt, baking soda, nutmeg, and cinnamon. Add to creamed mixture. Stir in coffee, nuts, and raisins. Chill at least 1 hour. Drop by teaspoons on greased cookie sheet. Bake 9 to 10 minutes. Makes 6 dozen cookies.

"Be eating one potato, peeling a second, have a third in your fist and your eye on a fourth." -*Old Irish saying*

P.E.I. DROP COOKIES

⅔ cup butter or margarine
1 cup brown sugar
1 egg, slightly beaten
2 tsp. vanilla
2 tsp. grated orange rind
1 cup grated carrot
½ cup mashed potato
1½ cups all-purpose flour
1½ tsp. baking powder
¼ tsp. salt

Preheat oven to 400 degrees. Cream butter and brown sugar. Add egg and vanilla and mix well. Beat in orange rind, carrot, and potato. Sift together flour, baking powder, and salt; add to the potato mixture. Drop by teaspoons onto a cookie sheet. Bake 10 to 12 minutes. Makes 40 cookies.

DOODLE DROPS

These are delicious fresh from the oven, especially with cold milk. This recipe is an adaptation of the Danish favorite, Snickerdoodles.

½ cup shortening
½ cup butter or margarine
1½ cups granulated sugar
2 eggs
½ cup mashed potato
2¾ cups all-purpose flour
2 tsp. cream of tartar
¼ tsp. salt
1 tsp. baking soda
2 tbsp. granulated sugar
2 tsp. cinnamon

Cream shortening and butter. Add sugar and blend well. Beat in eggs. Add potato, flour, cream of tartar, salt, and baking soda. Mix well. Chill until easy to handle. Preheat oven to 400 degrees. Roll dough in walnut-sized balls. Roll in a mixture of cinnamon and sugar. Bake 8 to 10 minutes. Cookies will feel soft on top but will firm up when cooled. Makes 4 dozen 2½" cookies.

OATMEAL COOKIES

1 cup all-purpose flour
1 cup quick cooking rolled oats
½ tsp. salt
½ tsp. cinnamon
¼ tsp. baking soda
½ cup mashed potato
2 tbsp. potato water or water
¾ cup butter or margarine
¾ cup brown sugar
¼ cup granulated sugar
1 egg, beaten
1 tsp. vanilla
½ cup chopped nuts
½ cup raisins

Preheat oven to 350 degrees. Combine flour, oats, salt, cinnamon, and baking soda. Set aside. Beat potato and water together until no lumps remain. Cream butter, sugars, and egg until light. Add vanilla. Add potato mixture and blend until well-mixed. Stir in dry ingredients until batter is smooth. Fold in nuts and raisins. Drop on lightly greased cookie sheet. Bake 15 to 20 minutes or until golden brown. Makes 4 dozen cookies.

SURPRISE COOKIES

1½ cups all-purpose flour
1½ tsp. baking powder
¼ tsp. salt
⅔ cup butter or margarine
1 cup brown sugar
1 egg
2 tsp. vanilla
½ cup mashed potato
½ cup nuts
2 tsp. orange rind
1 cup grated raw carrot
½ cup raisins

Preheat oven to 400 degrees. Combine flour, baking powder, and salt. Set aside. Cream butter, sugar, and egg until light. Add vanilla. Add potato and beat until no lumps remain. Blend in dry ingredients and mix until smooth. Fold in nuts, orange rind, carrot, and raisins. Drop by teaspoons onto an ungreased cookie sheet. Bake 10 to 12 minutes or until golden brown. Makes 4 dozen.

SOURDOUGH DROP COOKIES

1 cup shortening
2 cups firmly packed brown sugar
2 eggs
¾ cup Potato Sourdough (see Yeast Breads)
¾ cup mashed potato
2¼ cups all-purpose flour
1 tsp. salt
1 tsp. baking soda
1 cup raisins
1 tsp. vanilla

Preheat oven to 350 degrees. Cream shortening and sugar; add eggs, sourdough, and mashed potato. Sift flour, salt, and soda and add to mixture. Stir in raisins and vanilla. Drop on greased cookie sheets and bake 10 to 12 minutes. Makes 4 dozen cookies.

Note: Variations: Chopped nuts, chocolate chips, coconut, or cherries may be substituted for the raisins.

POTATO-PEANUT CRUNCHIES

If using salted peanuts in this recipe, omit the extra salt.

½ cup butter or margarine
¼ cup peanut butter
½ cup mashed potato (slightly warmed)
½ cup brown sugar
½ cup granulated sugar
1 egg
2 cups all-purpose flour
¼ tsp. salt
½ tsp. baking soda
½ tsp. cinnamon
⅛ tsp. cloves
½ cup finely chopped peanuts

Preheat oven to 400 degrees. Cream butter, peanut butter, and potato. Gradually blend in sugars and beat with electric mixer until light. Add egg and beat 1 minute longer. Combine dry ingredients; add to batter. Fold in chopped peanuts. Drop by teaspoons on ungreased cookie sheet and bake 10 to 12 minutes. Makes 4 dozen cookies.

Note: These cookies can be shaped in rolls, refrigerated, sliced, and baked when desired (dough will keep up to a week).

POTATO-CRANBERRY-APPLE DROP COOKIES

1 cup grated raw potato (use fine blade on grater)
1 cup chopped cranberries
1 cup apple, peeled and chopped or grated finely
1½ tsp. grated orange rind
½ cup butter or margarine
1 cup brown sugar
¾ cup granulated sugar
1 egg
¼ cup milk
2 cups all-purpose flour
1 tsp. baking powder
1 tsp. cinnamon
½ tsp. salt

Preheat oven to 375 degrees. Prepare potatoes, cranberries, apple, and orange rind. Cream butter and sugars; beat in egg and milk. Sift flour, baking powder, cinnamon, and salt. Stir into butter mixture until well-blended. Stir in orange rind, potato, apple, and cranberries. Drop by teaspoons onto greased cookie sheets. Bake 12 to 15 minutes. Makes 4 dozen cookies.

Note: Potatoes provide, per unit of land, more calories and more protein than any other major food crop—5 times as much food as corn, wheat, or soybeans.

THE POTATO COOKBOOK

POTATO-CHIPS COOKIES

This recipe is from the potato chip capital of the world: the United States. You will make these scrumptious cookies again and again. You may want to omit the extra salt if you use salted potato chips.

> 1 cup brown sugar
> 1 cup granulated sugar
> 1 cup shortening
> 2 eggs
> 1 tsp. vanilla
> 2 cups crushed potato chips
> 2 cups oatmeal
> 2 cups all-purpose flour
> 1 tsp. salt
> 1 tsp. baking soda

Preheat oven to 375 degrees. Cream sugars and shortening. Beat in eggs and vanilla. Add remaining ingredients and mix well. Drop by teaspoons on a baking sheet. Bake 10 to 15 minutes. Makes 6 dozen cookies.

". . . a rascally heap of sand and swamp . . . in the horrible Gulf of St. Lawrence . . . That lump of worthlessness bears nothing but potatoes." -*William Cobbet in his book,* The English Gardener, *writing about Prince Edward Island*

POTATO LEATHERBACKS

This is adapted from a recipe my mother made for lunch boxes when I was in school. Don't let the name fool you: these cookies are *not* leathery!

½ cup molasses
½ cup butter or margarine
⅓ cup brown sugar
1½ cups mashed potato
2 cups all-purpose flour
½ tsp. baking soda
½ tsp. ginger
1 tsp. cinnamon
½ tsp. salt
2 tsp. baking powder
1 cup raisins
Granulated sugar (optional)

Preheat oven to 375 degrees. Heat molasses and butter until butter melts. Add sugar; blend well. Stir in mashed potato. Sift dry ingredients. Stir raisins into dry ingredients and add to creamed mixture. Form dough in walnut-sized balls. Roll in granulated sugar. Bake on greased cookie sheet for 10 minutes. Makes 4 dozen cookies.

CHERRY PECAN SNOWBALLS

½ cup soft butter or margarine
½ cup icing sugar
¼ cup cold mashed potato
2 tbsp. milk
1 tsp. almond flavoring
¼ tsp. salt
1¾ cups all-purpose flour
½ cup chopped pecans
Maraschino cherries, drained and halved
Additional icing sugar

THE POTATO COOKBOOK

Preheat oven to 325 degrees. Cream butter and icing sugar. Blend in potato, milk, flavoring, and salt. Stir in flour and pecans. Mix well. Form dough in small balls with half a cherry inserted in the center. Bake on greased cookie sheet for 15 to 18 minutes. Cool slightly and roll in icing sugar. Makes 40 cookies.

SUGARED POTATO-CAKES

The origin of this recipe in unknown. It was previously published using vanilla sugar instead of vanilla in the CIP Women's Club cookbook from Peru.

5 tbsp. butter or margarine
1 tbsp. granulated sugar
1 tsp. vanilla
3 egg yolks
4 to 5 tbsp. sour cream
1 lb. potatoes (3 medium), cooked, peeled and finely grated, approx. 2 cups
2 cups sifted all-purpose flour
3 egg whites
Apricot or raspberry jam
Butter or margarine
3 tbsp. granulated sugar
1 tbsp. cinnamon

Cream together butter, sugar, vanilla, and egg yolks. Fold in sour cream. Into this, mix potato and flour. Quickly mix together to form a supple dough. Roll out to scarcely ½" thickness. Cut in 3" circles (be sure to have an even number of circles). Brush the edges of half the circles with egg white. Fill the center with thick jam. Cover with remaining rounds and press the edges together delicately. Brown on each side in butter in frying pan. Mix sugar and cinnamon. Roll cakes in cinnamon sugar while still warm. Makes 4 to 5 dozen cookies.

CHERRY-PECAN CHEWS

1 cup all-purpose flour
1 cup brown sugar, firmly packed
½ cup cold mashed potato
1 cup rolled oats
1 tsp. baking soda
¼ tsp. salt
½ cup butter or margarine
2 eggs, beaten
1 cup brown sugar, lightly packed
½ tsp. almond flavoring
2 tbsp. all-purpose flour
½ tsp. salt
1 cup coconut
1 cup well-drained maraschino cherries, halved
½ cup pecans, halved

Preheat oven to 350 degrees. Combine flour, 1 cup brown sugar, potato, rolled oats, baking soda, salt, and butter. Mix with a pastry blender until crumbly. Press in the bottom of a 13x9x2" cake pan. Bake 10 minutes. Remove from oven. Meanwhile, combine remaining ingredients, except for the pecans. Stir until well-blended and pour over cooked portion. Sprinkle pecan halves on top. Return to oven and bake for an additional 25 minutes. Cool thoroughly.

FROSTING

¼ cup butter or margarine
2 cups icing sugar
¼ tsp. almond extract
2 tbsp. maraschino cherry juice (approximate)

Blend butter and sugar; add flavoring and enough cherry juice to make a spreading consistency.

CRANBERRY CHRISTMAS SQUARES

⅔ cup shortening
⅔ cup warm mashed potato
⅔ cup icing sugar
1 tsp. vanilla
2 egg yolks
1¾ cups all-purpose flour

TOPPING

1 whole egg
2 egg whites
1 cup granulated sugar
⅓ cup all-purpose flour
¼ tsp. salt
1 tsp. baking powder
1 tsp. almond flavoring
⅓ cup raisins
⅓ cup chopped almonds
½ cup coconut
⅔ cup cranberry sauce

Preheat oven to 350 degrees. Cream shortening, potato, and icing sugar. Add vanilla and egg yolks and mix well. Stir in flour. Spread on a greased 9" square cake pan. Beat whole egg and egg whites until light. Add granulated sugar and continue beating until mixture resembles whipped cream. Fold in remaining ingredients, blending well. Pour over unbaked crust. Bake 40 to 45 minutes. Cool in pan. Ice with lemon-flavored icing.

Note: The largest potato grown in Britain to date weighed 7 pounds, 1 ounce. It was grown by J. H. East of Spalding in 1963.

CHOCOLATE-WALNUT POTATO SQUARES

I like to top these squares with small dollops of butter icing and pieces of chopped walnuts. They're attractive and tasty for special occasions.

BASE

⅓ cup shortening
⅓ cup warm mashed potato
⅓ cup icing sugar
½ tsp. vanilla
1 egg yolk
1 cup flour

TOPPING

1 egg white
1 whole egg
1 cup brown sugar
1 tbsp. flour
½ tsp. baking powder
¼ tsp. salt
1½ tbsp. cocoa
½ cup finely grated walnuts

Preheat oven to 375 degrees. Combine shortening, potato, icing sugar, vanilla, and egg yolk. Mix until creamy and well-blended. Stir in flour. Pat into an 8" square cake pan. Bake 10 minutes. Remove from oven. Reduce oven heat to 350 degrees. Prepare topping by beating egg white and whole egg until light and fluffy. Combine dry ingredients. (If cocoa is lumpy put it through a sieve.) Stir dry ingredients and walnuts into eggs. Spread over cooked base. Return to oven and bake 30 minutes. When cool, ice and decorate if desired.

Note: Variations: The base for these squares can be used for several variations of bar cookies. I particularly like to use this when baking for Christmas. I simply multiply the base recipe by the number of pans of squares I want to make and then use a variety of toppings.

FRUIT-AND-VEGETABLE-FUDGE SQUARES

These are moist and tender squares with a creamy fudge icing.

1 cup raisins
1 tsp. baking soda
1 cup boiling potato water
¼ cup shortening
1 cup granulated sugar
2 cups all-purpose flour
2 tsp. baking powder
¼ tsp. salt
1 tsp. vanilla
½ cup finely grated carrot
½ cup finely grated potato

Pour boiling water over raisins and baking soda. Cool to lukewarm. Preheat oven to 350 degrees. Grease and flour a 9x13" cake pan. Cream shortening; add sugar and raisin mixture. Sift dry ingredients. Add to creamed mixture along with vanilla and grated vegetables. Mix well. Spread in prepared pan and bake 30 minutes. Cool thoroughly.

FUDGE ICING

3 tbsp. butter or margarine
3 tbsp. brown sugar
2 tbsp. cream or evaporated milk
1 tsp. vanilla or desired flavoring
Icing sugar

Heat butter, sugar, and cream until butter and sugar are melted. Add vanilla or desired flavoring and enough icing sugar to make a spreading consistency. Spread on cool cake. Decorate with walnuts if desired.

CALIFORNIA POTATO-DATE SQUARES

1 medium potato, peeled and boiled in 1¼ cups water
1 cup chopped dates
1 tsp. baking soda
¼ cup shortening
1 cup granulated sugar
1 egg
1 tsp. vanilla
1¾ cups flour
¼ tsp. salt

TOPPING

4 tbsp. melted butter or margarine
4 tbsp. cream or evaporated milk
½ cup brown sugar
1 cup coconut
1 tsp. vanilla

Drain water from cooked potato and reserve 1 cup to pour over dates. Let dates, potato water, and baking soda sit until they cool to room temperature. Mash potato; cool to room temperature. Preheat oven to 350 degrees. Grease and lightly flour a 9x13" cake pan. Cream shortening; add sugar and egg. Beat well. Stir in vanilla and mashed potatoes. Add flour and salt alternately with date and water mixture. Mix well. Bake in prepared pan for 30 minutes. Meanwhile, combine topping ingredients. When cake is finished baking, remove from oven and spread topping over cake. Return to oven and bake until brown or put under the broiler for 3 to 4 minutes.

Note: Nutritionists agree that the diet of nineteenth-century Ireland, 5 pounds of potatoes and 1 quart of milk per day, provided all nutrients essential to a human being.

BUTTERSCOTCH CONGO BARS

⅔ cup soft shortening or margarine
⅔ cup warm mashed potato
2 cups brown sugar
1 tsp. vanilla
3 eggs
¼ tsp. salt
1½ tsp. baking powder
1¾ cups all-purpose flour
2 cups butterscotch chips

Preheat oven to 350 degrees. Grease a 9x13" cake pan and line with waxed paper. Cream shortening and potato. Add brown sugar and blend until light. Beat in vanilla and eggs. Sift salt, baking powder, and flour; stir into other mixture. Spread in prepared pan. Sprinkle with butterscotch chips, pressing them lightly into batter with back of a spoon. Bake 25 to 30 minutes.

CHERRY-ALMOND BARS

Prepare and cook base (see page 120). Top with the following:

1 egg white
1 whole egg
1 cup brown sugar
½ tsp. almond flavoring
½ tsp. baking powder
1 tbsp. all-purpose flour
½ cup finely chopped blanched almonds
½ cup finely chopped candied cherries

Beat egg white and whole egg. Add sugar and flavoring; mix well. Stir in remaining ingredients. Pour over cooked base. Return to oven and bake 30 minutes. Frost with butter icing.

POTATO MAPLE-WALNUT DREAM BARS

These are rich and delicious!

⅓ cup shortening
⅓ cup warm mashed potato
⅓ cup icing sugar
½ tsp. vanilla
1 egg yolk
1 cup all-purpose flour

TOPPING

½ cup brown sugar
½ cup Potato Maple Syrup (see Miscellaneous)
2 eggs, beaten
1 tbsp. all-purpose flour
½ tsp. baking powder
¼ tsp. salt
½ tsp. vanilla
½ cup coconut
1 cup grated walnuts

Preheat oven to 400 degrees. Beat shortening, potato, and icing sugar until well-blended. Add vanilla and egg yolk. Mix well. Stir in flour. Pat into a greased 8" square cake pan. Bake 10 minutes. Remove from oven. Reduce oven heat to 350 degrees. Combine brown sugar, maple syrup, and beaten eggs. Beat until light and creamy. Add remaining ingredients. Mix until well-blended. Pour over slightly cooled base. Return to oven and bake 20 to 25 minutes. Cool in pan. May be frosted when cool with butter icing.

COFFEE-NUT POTATO BARS

1 medium potato, peeled and cubed
⅔ cup potato water
1 tbsp. instant coffee
½ cup butter or margarine
2 cups brown sugar
2 eggs
1 tsp. vanilla
2 cups all-purpose flour
1 tsp. salt
2 tsp. baking powder

Boil potato until tender. Drain, reserving cooking water. Mash potato and cool slightly. Combine ⅔ cup of cooking water with instant coffee; set aside. Preheat oven to 350 degrees. Grease a 9x13" cake pan and line bottom with waxed paper. Cream butter, potato, and brown sugar. Add eggs and beat until light and fluffy. Sift and stir in dry ingredients alternately with ½ cup coffee mixture. Save remaining coffee for frosting. Spread in prepared pan and bake for 30 to 35 minutes.

FROSTING

2 tbsp. butter or margarine
2 cups icing sugar
1 tbsp. cocoa
1 tsp. vanilla
Reserved coffee, about 2 to 3 tbsp.

Combine butter, icing sugar, cocoa, vanilla, and enough coffee to make a spreading consistency. Spread over cooled squares.

Note: Pioneer children brought their potatoes to school and gave them to the caretaker or the teacher. He would carve each child's initials in their "tater" and put them on the stove. At recess the children would have a tasty, healthy snack.

CAKES

I have always associated cakes with happiness. Traditionally cakes were served for company on special occasions—Christmas, Easter, birthdays, weddings, christenings, or when Grandma came to visit. There's a cake for everyone and for every occasion. World leaders and celebrities have cakes named for them—Queen Elizabeth Cake, Lord and Lady Baltimore Cakes, to name a few.

For a special day, or just because you feel good, why not make someone happy by baking a cake.

Remember when baking cakes to grease the bottom of the pans, but not the sides. Your cake will have smooth level top. It is not easy to climb a greased pan. Also, when recipe calls for mashed potatoes be sure they are very finely mashed or riced—you don't want any lumps!

Note: In some parts of the world, potatoes are a luxury. Philippine housewives sometimes top off their grocery bags with potatoes to show they are from an affluent family.

BOILED RAISIN CAKE

During World War II, when fruit and nuts were not available, this recipe was used to make an economical fruit cake. I like to add a few candied cherries and mixed fruit and use this recipe for my Dark Fruit Cake each Christmas. It is not nearly as rich as the traditional fruit cake and can be made almost at the last minute.

2 cups boiling potato water
2 cups granulated sugar
½ cup butter or margarine
½ cup lard
2 cups raisins
2 tsp. cinnamon
1 tsp. cloves
1 tsp. salt
2 tsp. baking soda
3½ cups all-purpose flour
2 tsp. baking powder
½ cup finely mashed potato

Grease and line a 10" tube pan with 2 layers of waxed paper or 1 layer of brown paper that has been greased on the inside. In a medium saucepan combine potato water, sugar, butter, lard, raisins, cinnamon, cloves, and salt. Bring to a boil and simmer 1 minute. Remove from heat; add 2 tsp. baking soda and cool to room temperature. Preheat oven to 350 degrees. Add remaining ingredients. Blend well. Pour into prepared pan. Bake for approximately 1½ hours. A small container of water in the oven will make a moister cake.

Note: Fruit Cake Variation: Add 2 to 3 cups candied citron, cherries, or mixed fruit to the first mixture before boiling.

CHOCOLATE POTATO LAYER CAKE

½ cup milk
½ cup plus 2 level tbsp. cocoa
1 cup plus 1½ tbsp. butter or margarine
1¾ cups granulated sugar
1 cup hot mashed potato
4 egg yolks
2 cups sifted all-purpose flour
1 tbsp. baking powder
¼ tsp. salt
1 tsp. vanilla
4 egg whites
¼ cup granulated sugar

Preheat oven to 350 degrees. Grease and flour three 8" cake pans. Heat milk slowly in a saucepan. Add cocoa and 1½ tbsp. butter. Stir until melted and mix well. Cool. Cream remaining butter with 1¾ cups sugar until light and fluffy. Combine chocolate mixture with potato and add to creamed mixture. Beat in egg yolks. Sift together flour, baking powder, and salt; stir into batter. Add vanilla. Beat egg whites until stiff, adding the ¼ cup sugar gradually. Fold into batter. Pour into prepared pans. Bake for 30 minutes. Cool on racks and frost as desired or sprinkle with icing sugar.

Note: The early Parliamentarians in England used potato flour as wig powder.

CHERRY CHOCOLATE CAKE

½ cup shortening
⅔ cup mashed potato
1½ cups granulated sugar
3 eggs
2 squares unsweetened chocolate, melted over hot water
2 cups all-purpose flour
¾ tsp. baking powder
¾ tsp. salt
1¼ cups sour milk or buttermilk
¼ cup maraschino cherry juice
⅔ cup maraschino cherries, drained and halved

Preheat oven to 375 degrees. Grease and flour two 9" cake pans. Cream together shortening, potato, and sugar. Add eggs, one at a time, beating well after each addition. Stir in melted chocolate. Sift flour, baking soda, baking powder, and salt at least twice. Stir cherry juice into sour milk. Add dry ingredients to batter alternating with milk mixture, making several additions, beginning and ending with dry ingredients. Stir in cherries. Bake in prepared pans for 35 minutes. Cool on racks. Frost with Butter Cream Icing flavored with almond or cherry.

BUTTER CREAM ICING

3 tbsp. soft butter or margarine
Pinch salt
½ tsp. vanilla, lemon, or almond flavoring
2 cups icing sugar
2 to 2½ tsp. warm milk

Cream butter; add salt and flavoring. Blend in icing sugar alternately with milk. Beat until smooth. For a layer cake, use a double recipe.

EASY BLACK FOREST CAKE

This cake also makes a delicious plain chocolate cake when iced with any desired frosting.

3 squares unsweetened chocolate
½ cup butter or margarine (soften but do not melt)
½ cup mashed potato
2¼ cups firmly packed brown sugar
3 large eggs
2½ cups all-purpose flour
2 tsp. baking soda
½ tsp. salt
½ cup buttermilk
1 cup boiling clear potato water
Cherry pie filling (19-oz. can)
Whipped cream or whipped topping
Chocolate curls (shaved semi-sweet chocolate)

Preheat oven to 350 degrees. Grease and flour three 8" cake pans or one 13x9" cake pan. (I prefer oblong pan as 3 layers makes a very high cake.) Cream melted chocolate, butter, potato, and brown sugar until well-blended. Add eggs one at a time, beating after each addition. Sift together flour, baking soda, and salt. Add dry ingredients to mixture alternately with buttermilk. Blend well. Fold in boiling potato water. Pour batter into prepared pans. Bake 25 minutes for layers and 40 to 45 minutes for oblong pan. When cool, cover with cherry pie filling. Spread with whipped cream and sprinkle with chocolate curls for garnish, if desired.

CHOCOLATE-PECAN CAKE

1 cup pecans, finely chopped
2 cups all-purpose flour
¾ tsp. baking soda
¼ tsp. salt
2 cups granulated sugar
¾ cup butter or margarine
2 tsp. vanilla
4 eggs
¾ cup mashed potato
3 oz. unsweetened chocolate, melted over hot water
⅔ cup buttermilk

Preheat oven to 350 degrees. Grease a 13x9" cake pan and line with waxed paper. Toss pecans in ¼ cup flour. Sift remaining flour, baking soda, and salt. Cream butter and sugar. Add vanilla and eggs, adding one egg at a time and mixing well after each addition. Stir in potato and chocolate. Add sifted dry ingredients alternately with buttermilk, beginning and ending with dry ingredients. Fold in pecans. Bake 50 to 55 minutes. Cool.

FROSTING

⅔ cup melted butter or margarine
¼ cup milk
3 tbsp. cocoa
2½ to 3 cups icing sugar
1 tsp. vanilla

Combine melted butter, milk, and vanilla. Sift cocoa with 2 cups icing sugar. Add to mixture and beat well. Add extra icing sugar if necessary to make a spreading consistency.

FESTIVE CAKE

This is a moist rich cake with that *ever-popular chocolate flavor.*

2 cups granulated sugar
¾ cup butter, margarine, or shortening
4 eggs, separated
2 cups all-purpose flour
2 tsp. baking powder
1 tsp. cinnamon
1 tsp. nutmeg
¼ tsp. salt
¾ cup cocoa
1 cup mashed potato
½ cup milk
1 tsp. vanilla
1 cup raisins
1 cup chopped walnuts

Preheat oven to 350 degrees. Grease and flour 10" tube pan. Cream sugar and butter. Add egg yolks and beat thoroughly. Sift together flour, baking powder, cinnamon, nutmeg, cocoa, and salt. Coat raisins in small portion of flour mixture. Add potato to creamed mixture. Add flour mixture alternately with milk, beating after each addition, beginning and ending with flour. Add vanilla, raisins, and nuts. Fold in stiffly beaten egg whites. Bake for 1 hour or until toothpick inserted in center comes out dry. Cool, and frost if desired.

Note: Potatoes can be used in various ways and are considered one of the world's most versatile foods. Maybe this is why a "jack-of-all-trades" in India is called "alu," meaning potato.

POTATO POUND CAKE

Beating for the specified amount of time is important for this cake's success. Pound cake is better if it has aged 1 or 2 days.

1 cup soft butter or margarine
1 cup granulated sugar
1 tsp. grated lemon rind
1 tbsp. lemon juice
4 large eggs
⅜ cup finely mashed potato
¼ tsp. nutmeg
¼ tsp. baking powder
1⅝ cups all-purpose flour

Preheat oven to 325 degrees. Grease and lightly flour a 9x5x3" loaf pan. Cream butter thoroughly (1 minute). Add sugar gradually, creaming well after each addition (10 minutes). Mix in the lemon rind and juice (30 seconds). Beat in the eggs one at a time, beating for 1½ minutes with each egg. Add potato; mix well. Sift together and stir in the dry ingredients. Mix just until smooth (about 1 minute). Pour into prepared pan. Bake for 30 minutes, then reduce heat to 300 degrees and bake approximately 1 hour. Cool. Slice thinly and serve plain.

SPONGE CAKE

Try this version of an old favorite, this time with potato flour. Again, be sure not to substitute the flour.

¾ cup sugar
½ cup potato flour
1 tsp. baking powder
¼ tsp. salt
4 egg whites
4 egg yolks
½ tsp. lemon juice

Preheat oven to 350 degrees. Sift sugar, set aside. Sift flour with baking powder and salt. Beat egg whites until stiff, add 4 tbsp. of the sugar; set aside. Beat egg yolks until thick and lemon-colored. Beat in remaining sugar and lemon juice. Fold egg-white mixture into yolks. Mix in dry ingredients. Cut and fold into egg mixture. Do not beat. (Light mixing and folding will help avoid breaking air bubbles.) Bake in an ungreased 10" tube pan for 40 minutes.

CHERRY-POTATO POUND CAKE

Be sure to beat this batter the specified amount of time. This makes a moist, attractive cake for afternoon tea and a nice alternative to fruit cakes at Christmas.

> **1 cup soft butter or margarine**
> **1 cup fine granulated sugar**
> **1 tsp. grated lemon rind**
> **1 tbsp. freshly squeezed lemon juice**
> **4 large eggs**
> **½ cup riced potato**
> **½ tsp. almond extract**
> **¼ tsp. double-acting baking powder**
> **1½ cups presifted all-purpose flour**
> **1 cup candied cherries (red and green) halved**
> **2 tbsp. all-purpose flour to lightly coat cherries**

Grease a 9x5x3" loaf pan and line with waxed paper. Cream butter for 1 minute. Gradually add sugar, creaming well after each addition. Cream 10 minutes after last sugar is added. Mix in lemon rind and juice and beat 30 seconds. Beat in eggs one at a time, beating for 1 minute with each egg. Add potato and almond extract. Mix well. Sift dry ingredients. Gradually add to other mixture; mix just until smooth. Fold in floured cherries and pour into prepared pan. Let sit while preheating oven to 325 degrees. Bake for 30 minutes; reduce heat to 300 degrees and bake approximately 1 hour longer. Cool thoroughly before slicing. Slice thinly and serve plain.

POTATO-APPLESAUCE CAKE

Combinations of potatoes and applesauce have long been favorites at home and abroad. Here they team up with oatmeal and spice to make a deliciously moist cake. Frost with Butter Cream Frosting and sprinkle with chopped nuts, if desired. My family likes this cake served hot with whipped cream for dessert.

½ cup butter or margarine
1 cup granulated sugar
1 egg
1½ cups all-purpose flour
1 tsp. soda
½ tsp. salt
1 tsp. cinnamon
½ tsp. cloves
⅔ cup grated potato (grated medium-coarse)
1 cup sweetened applesauce
½ cup chopped walnuts
1 cup rolled oats

Preheat oven to 350 degrees. Grease and flour an 8" square cake pan. Beat butter until creamy; add sugar and egg, mixing well. Sift together all dry ingredients. Stir into the creamed mixture. Blend well. Combine potato, applesauce, and chopped nuts. Stir into batter along with rolled oats. Pour into prepared pan and bake in preheated oven for 45 minutes. Let stand in pan 5 minutes before removing to a wire rack to cool. Frost if desired with Butter Cream Icing.

"A diet that consists predominantly of rice leads to the use of opium, just as a diet which consists predominantly of potatoes leads to the use of liquor." -F. W. Nietzche

POTATO-CHERRY-WALNUT LAYER CAKE

This light fluffy cake combines the flavors of maraschino cherries and walnuts.

4 egg whites
⅓ cup granulated sugar
2 cups all-purpose flour
3 tsp. baking powder
¾ tsp. salt
¾ cup shortening
1½ cups granulated sugar
1 cup mashed potato
4 egg yolks
1 tsp. vanilla
1 cup milk
½ cup maraschino cherries, chopped finely
½ cup walnuts, grated or chopped in a blender

Preheat oven to 350 degrees. Grease and flour three 8" cake pans on the bottom only (do not grease the sides of the pan). Beat egg whites until thick and foamy. Gradually add ⅓ cup sugar and beat until stiff. Set aside. Sift together flour, baking powder, and salt. In a large mixing bowl cream shortening and gradually add remaining sugar; blend well. Add potato, egg yolks, and vanilla. Beat until light and fluffy. Alternately add dry ingredients and milk, beginning and ending with dry ingredients. Fold in cherries and nuts along with the last addition of flour. Mix well. Gently fold in stiffly beaten egg whites. Put in prepared pans. Bake for 30 minutes. Ice with Butter Cream Icing.

Note: The potato industry in Canada dates back to 1623 when a small patch was grown at Port Royal, Nova Scotia.

VELVET NUT CAKE

Mashed potato gives this cake a beautiful, velvety texture.

1¾ cups all-purpose flour
1 tsp. baking soda
½ tsp. nutmeg
1 tsp. cinnamon
½ tsp. salt
1 cup mashed potato
1 cup buttermilk
¾ cup shortening
1½ cups brown sugar
3 eggs, separated
¾ cup chopped walnuts

Preheat oven to 350 degrees. Grease and flour two 8" cake pans. Combine flour, baking soda, nutmeg, cinnamon, and salt. Set aside. Beat potato and buttermilk together until no lumps remain. Cream shortening, sugar, and egg yolks until light. Add vanilla. Blend in dry ingredients gradually, alternating with potato/milk mixture, beginning and ending with dry ingredients. Fold in nuts and stiffly beaten egg whites. Pour batter into pans and bake 45 minutes, until a toothpick inserted in center comes out dry.

ORANGE POTATO CAKE

This is a delicate light cake with a subtle orange flavor. It's excellent for gluten-free diets. Be sure to follow the exact method of preparation and to use potato flour.

4 eggs
1 cup granulated sugar
½ cup potato flour
1 tsp. baking powder
½ tsp. salt
2 tbsp. orange juice
Grated rind of half an orange

Preheat oven to 325 degrees. Grease and line with waxed paper an 8" square cake pan. Beat eggs on high speed with a mixer until thick and smooth; gradually add sugar, beating until mixture resembles whipped cream. Sift together potato flour, baking powder, and salt. Blend into egg mixture. Add orange juice and rind and mix thoroughly. Spread in cake pan. Bake for 15 minutes; increase heat to 350 degrees and bake an additional 15 minutes or until cake is firm. Cool on cake rack. Do not open oven door during the first 25 minutes of baking as the cake will fall easily.

PIONEER POTATO CAKE

You cannot substitute the potato flour and achieve the same results with this recipe. Potato flour can be obtained at most health food stores. A light and delicious cake, it is excellent served with strawberries and cream.

¾ cup potato flour
1 tsp. baking powder
½ tsp. salt
4 eggs
¾ cup granulated sugar
1 tsp. vanilla
1 tsp. lemon juice

Preheat oven to 350 degrees. Sift together flour, baking powder, and salt. Mix eggs and sugar in a mixing bowl. Set bowl in a larger bowl containing hot water. Beat with an electric mixer until mixture is lukewarm. Remove from hot water and beat for 6 to 8 minutes. (Mixture is very light and fluffy, resembling whipped cream.) Add flavoring. Gradually fold in dry ingredients. Pour into an ungreased 8" tube pan. Bake for 40 minutes. Invert pan to cool.

DESSERTS

Every cook at some time or another wants to show off—to do something daring and dramatic. Here is your chance to serve potatoes for dessert. In this chapter you will find recipes for pies (North America's favorite dessert) as well as shortcakes, puddings, and gingerbread.

Whether plain or fancy, desserts are the crowning glory of any table.

POTATO MAPLE-WALNUT PIE

Pastry for single-crust 9" pie
½ cup butter or margarine
1 cup brown sugar
1 cup Potato Maple Syrup (see Miscellaneous)
4 eggs, slightly beaten
Pinch salt
1 tsp. vanilla
1 cup chopped walnuts

Preheat oven to 375 degrees. Line pie plate with pastry. Combine all ingredients. Mix well. Bake 40 minutes, until center is firm. Serves 6.

Note: Variation: Try Potato Pecan Pie, substituting pecans for walnuts.

POTATO SYRUP PIE

Pastry for single-crust 9" pie
¾ cup raisins
2 tbsp. butter or margarine
1 egg
¾ cup Potato Maple Syrup (see Miscellaneous)
¾ cup brown sugar
½ cup peanut butter
¼ tsp. salt
1 tsp. vanilla
½ cup evaporated milk

Preheat oven to 400 degrees. Line pie plate with pastry. Sprinkle with raisins. Beat butter, egg, syrup, sugar, peanut butter, salt, vanilla, and milk with electric mixer. Pour over raisins. Bake 15 minutes; reduce heat to 325 degrees and bake 45 minutes. Cool completely. Serve with whipped cream. Serves 6.

Note: This filling can be used for tarts (makes 12 tarts).

MID-WINTER PIE

This is a combination of apples, potatoes, and cranberries that is sure to be a favorite. Serve with ice cream or whipped cream.

Pastry for double-crust 9" pie
1 cup grated raw potato (medium-fine)
1½ cups peeled apple, coarsely grated
1½ cups raw cranberries
½ cup water
⅔ cup granulated sugar
2 tbsp. all-purpose flour
½ cup corn syrup or Potato Maple Syrup (see Miscellaneous)
⅛ tsp. salt
1 tsp. grated orange rind

In medium saucepan cook potato, apple, and cranberries in water until cranberries pop. Watch closely as this mixture will burn easily. Stir in sugar. Remove from heat, cover, and cool to room temperature. Preheat oven to 425 degrees. Combine flour, syrup, salt, and orange rind. Stir into potato mixture. Pour into pastry-lined pie plate. Cover with lattice top. Bake 40 minutes. Serves 6.

LEMONY POTATO PIE

An unusually tasty early American dessert, this pie is very rich. Serve with whipped cream.

Pastry for single-crust 9" pie
4 medium potatoes, peeled and sliced thinly
1½ cups granulated sugar
Juice of 1 lemon
¼ cup potato water
½ cup dark brown sugar
1 tbsp. butter or margarine

Boil potato slices in water until barely tender. Remove from water with a slotted spoon, taking care not to break them; save potato water. Stir sugar, lemon juice, and ¼ cup reserved potato water in saucepan. Simmer for 5 minutes, stirring occasionally. Carefully add the potato slices to the lemon-sugar syrup. Bring to a boil. Remove from heat and cool. Preheat oven to 425 degrees. Line a 9" pie plate with pastry. Arrange cooled potato slices over the crust and pour syrup over. Sprinkle with brown sugar, dot with butter, and bake 15 minutes; reduce heat to 350 degrees and bake 30 to 35 minutes longer. Serve at room temperature or chilled. Serves 6.

LEMON-CUSTARD POTATO PIE

Pastry for single-crust 9" pie (partially cooked for 6 to 8 minutes)
½ cup warm mashed potato
2 tbsp. butter or margarine
2 egg whites
¾ cup granulated sugar
2 egg yolks
Juice of ½ lemon
1 tbsp. finely grated lemon rind
½ cup milk

Preheat oven to 400 degrees. Whip potato and butter with electric mixer until smooth. Cool. Beat egg whites until stiff peaks form. To potato/butter mixture add sugar, egg yolks, lemon juice, lemon rind, and milk. Blend thoroughly. Fold in egg whites. Put in partially cooked pastry shell. Bake 25 to 30 minutes. Serves 6.

IRISH APPLE PIE

This is a delicious apple dessert from Ireland. The pastry is not as firm as regular pastry. Be sure to grease the pie pan.

2 cups hot mashed potato
1 tbsp. butter or margarine
⅛ tsp. cinnamon
⅛ tsp. ginger
1 tbsp. brown sugar
¼ cup all-purpose flour
4 cups thinly sliced apples
2 tbsp. brown sugar
1 tsp. melted butter or margarine
1 tsp. granulated sugar

Preheat oven to 375 degrees. Combine potato, butter, cinnamon, ginger, and brown sugar. Mix well. Blend in flour. Reserve ¾ cup for top of the pie. On a sheet of waxed paper, pat the remaining dough into a circle slightly larger than a 9" pie plate. Place a well-greased pie plate over dough. Lift and invert the dough into the pan. Remove waxed paper. Arrange apple slices over potato mixture. Sprinkle with 2 tbsp. brown sugar. Pat remaining ¾ cup of potato mixture onto a 9" circle of waxed paper. Invert over pie. Peel off paper, crimp and seal around edges of dough around pie. Cut a vent in the center of the pie. Bake 45 to 50 minutes. Brush top with 1 tsp. melted butter and sprinkle with granulated sugar a few minutes before removing from oven. Serve hot with whipped cream. Serves 6.

MINCEMEAT-AND-POTATO PIE

This is a delicious mincemeat pie with creamy potato topping.

Pastry for single-crust 9" pie
1 cup mashed potato
1 cup evaporated milk
½ cup brown sugar
1 egg, slightly beaten
½ tsp. salt
¼ tsp. cinnamon
¼ tsp. ginger
1 tsp. grated lemon rind
1 tbsp. butter or margarine
2 cups prepared mincemeat*

Preheat oven to 450 degrees. Combine potato, milk, brown sugar, egg, salt, cinnamon, ginger, and lemon rind. Cook over low heat for 3 to 4 minutes, stirring constantly (until slightly thickened). Stir in butter. Put mincemeat in bottom of pastry-lined pie plate; top with potato mixture. Bake for 15 minutes. Reduce heat to 350 degrees and bake 30 minutes longer. Serves 6.

*Green tomato mincemeat works, too.

POTATO MAPLE-BUTTER TARTS

Pastry for 12 tart shells
Boiling water or potato water
½ cup raisins
½ cup butter or margarine
½ cup brown sugar
¼ tsp. salt
½ cup Potato Maple Syrup (see Miscellaneous)
1 beaten egg
½ tsp. vanilla
Few drops lemon juice

Preheat oven to 350 degrees. Pour boiling water over raisins and let soak until edges turn white. Drain. Meanwhile, cream butter, add sugar, and mix well. Beat in remaining ingredients. Add raisins. Fill tart shells ⅔ full. Bake 20 minutes. Do not let filling boil. Makes 12 tarts.

POTATO-RHUBARB DELIGHT

This tangy rhubarb has a rich and delicious biscuit topping.

> **3 cups chopped rhubarb**
> **½ cup granulated sugar**
> **1 cup all-purpose flour**
> **1½ tsp. baking powder**
> **¼ tsp. salt**
> **¼ cup granulated sugar**
> **⅜ cup butter or margarine**
> **1 cup sieved or riced cooked potato**

Preheat oven to 400 degrees. Wash rhubarb well and place in a 9" pie plate. Add sugar and bake for 15 minutes. (Dot with butter and add a pinch of salt if desired.) Meanwhile, combine flour, baking powder, salt, and sugar. Cut in butter. Stir in potato. Knead to form a dough. Roll out to ½" thickness on a lightly floured board. Cut in circles with a biscuit cutter. Remove fruit from oven. Drain off juice and save. Pour back ¼ cup of juice; discard remaining juice or save to use later in muffins or a jellied salad. Cover fruit with circles of biscuit. Bake 15 minutes or until golden brown. Serve hot with sweetened whipped cream. Serves 6.

THE POTATO COOKBOOK

POTATO GINGERBREAD

This gingerbread keeps well. It may be served with whipped cream or Foamy Egg Sauce (*see* Centennial Pudding). Raisins may also be added to the mixture.

⅝ **cup shortening**
½ **cup granulated sugar**
2 **eggs**
1 **cup molasses**
½ **cup finely mashed potato**
2⅛ **cups all-purpose flour**
2 **tsp. baking powder**
1 **tsp. cinnamon**
1 **tsp. ginger**
½ **tsp. salt**
1 **cup hot potato water or water**

Preheat oven to 350 degrees. Lightly grease and flour a 9x9" cake pan. Cream shortening; add sugar and cream together until well-blended. Add eggs and molasses and beat thoroughly. Blend in potato. Sift together flour, baking powder, cinnamon, ginger, and salt. Add to the potato mixture and beat only until smooth. Add the hot water and mix until well-blended. Bake 40 minutes. Serves 9.

Note: The headmaster of a cooking school in Dardilly, France, requires each of his students to prepare sixty potato dishes before graduation.

GRANDMA'S APPLE CAKE

This is a delicious dessert served with whipped cream or cooled and iced with a butter icing.

¾ cup butter or margarine
⅔ cup sugar
2 eggs, beaten
⅔ cup hot mashed potato
1¾ cups all-purpose flour
½ tsp. salt
1 tbsp. baking powder
½ tsp. cinnamon
2 medium cooking apples (peel and slice thinly when ready to use*)

Preheat oven to 350 degrees. Grease and flour an 8" square cake pan. Cream butter, sugar, and eggs until light. Blend in potato. Combine flour, salt, baking powder, and cinnamon. Fold into butter mixture, blending until well-mixed. Fold in sliced apples. Pour batter into prepared pan and bake 45 to 50 minutes.

*Do not peel apples ahead as they will darken.

Note: A "Potato Monument" stands at the site of a ruined castle in Hirchhorn, in the Neckar Valley. The inscription reads: "To God and Francis Drake, who brought to Europe for the everlasting benefit of the poor—the potato."

ALL-SEASONS SHORTCAKE

Strawberries, raspberries, blueberries, and other fruits such as apples, peaches, and rhubarb may be used with this recipe. This recipe comes from the P.E.I. Potato Marketing Board.

1 cup all-purpose flour
2 tsp. baking powder
¼ tsp. salt
¼ cup granulated sugar
⅜ cup butter or margarine
1 cup mashed potato
¾ cup berries
¼ cup sugar
½ cup whipping cream

Preheat oven to 400 degrees. Combine flour, baking powder, salt, and sugar in a mixing bowl. Cut in butter until mixture is crumbly. Stir in potato. Knead to form a dough and roll out to 1" thickness on a lightly floured board. Cut into circles with a biscuit cutter. Bake 15 minutes or until golden brown. Mash ⅔ cup berries (save a few for garnish). Strain the liquid (especially important with raspberries). Add 3 tbsp. sugar to berries. When biscuits are cool, split in two. Place 1½ tbsp. berries on bottom of each biscuit. Whip cream with about 2 tsp. sugar. Spread cream on biscuit and cover with the biscuit top. Garnish with a small amount of whipped cream and a few whole berries. Serves 6.

Note: An annual festival in O'Leary, Prince Edward Island, is held in July to coincide with the times when potato fields are in bloom. It is called the "Potato Blossom Festival."

CENTENNIAL PUDDING (WITH FOAMY EGG SAUCE)

A recipe from the P.E.I. Potato Marketing Board, this is definitely a celebration-day pudding. May be cooked ahead and reheated for serving.

½ cup ground suet
½ cup brown sugar
½ cup molasses
1½ cups grated carrot
1 cup grated raw potato
1 cup all-purpose flour
1 tsp. baking soda
½ tsp. salt
1 tsp. cinnamon
⅛ tsp. ground cloves
½ tsp. nutmeg
½ tsp. allspice
1 cup chopped raisins
⅓ cup chopped candied orange peel or citron

Combine suet, sugar, molasses, grated carrot, and potato. Mix well. Sift together flour, baking soda, salt, cinnamon, cloves, nutmeg, and allspice. Add to first mixture and stir well. Add raisins and chopped fruit. Fill a well-greased 1½-quart pudding mold ⅔ full. Cover lightly and steam for 3 to 3½ hours. Serve with Foamy Egg Sauce. Serves 10 to 12.

FOAMY EGG SAUCE

4 egg yolks
1 cup icing sugar
¾ tsp. vanilla or rum flavoring
Pinch salt
1½ cups whipping cream

Beat egg yolks, icing sugar, flavoring, and salt. Whip cream; fold into mixture. Chill. Stir before serving. Makes 4 cups.

STEAMED POTATO PUDDING (WITH LEMON SAUCE)

This is from the kitchen of Pauline Essery, Summerside, P.E.I.

½ cup shortening
1 cup granulated sugar
1 cup grated raw potato
1¼ cups grated raw carrot
1 cup all-purpose flour
1 tsp. baking soda
1 tsp. salt
1 tsp. cinnamon
½ tsp. cloves
1 cup raisins
⅓ cup candied citron peel

Cream shortening and sugar. Add vegetables. Mix dry ingredients and fruit. Add to the above mixture and blend well. Press lightly into a greased pudding mold. Cover loosely with tin foil and steam for 2¼ hours. Serve warm with Lemon Sauce. (The pudding also freezes well; it will keep up to six months in a freezer. Thaw and re-heat in 325-degree oven for 20 minutes, or steam for the same length of time.)

LEMON SAUCE

¼ cup granulated sugar
1 tbsp. cornstarch
Few grains salt
1 cup cold water (can use leftover potato water)
2 tbsp. lemon juice
2 tbsp. butter or margarine

Mix dry ingredients; add cold water. Cook over low heat until thickened, stirring constantly. Add lemon juice and butter. Pour over pudding. Serves 10 to 12.

POTATO CHRISTMAS PUDDING
(WITH BROWN SUGAR RUM SAUCE)

Adapted from the CIP international potato cookbook published in Peru by the International Potato Centre Women's Club (Las Damas del CIP), this dessert can be made in advance and reheated in the oven or in a steamer.

½ cup shortening
1 cup granulated sugar
1 cup grated raw potato
1½ cups grated raw carrot
1 cup all-purpose flour
1 tsp. baking soda
1 tsp. salt
1 tsp. cinnamon
½ tsp. cloves
½ cup seedless raisins
½ cup diced candied fruit

Cream together shortening and sugar. Add potato and carrot. Sift dry ingredients and combine with raisins and fruit. Mix all ingredients together. Fill greased 1½-quart pudding mold ¾ full; cover lightly with tin foil. Steam 2½ hours. Unmold. Serve hot with Brown Sugar Rum Sauce. Serves 10 to 12.

BROWN SUGAR RUM SAUCE

¾ cup brown sugar
Dash salt
1½ tbsp. all-purpose flour
1½ cups boiling water or potato water
2 tbsp. margarine or butter
⅓ cup rum

Mix sugar, salt, and flour in a saucepan. Add boiling water slowly. Cook and stir over direct heat until smooth and slightly thickened. Simmer 5 minutes. Remove from heat and add butter and rum. Stir until well-mixed. Pour hot over pudding.

BAKED LEMON-AND-POTATO PUDDING

This is a cake-type pudding with a rich lemon sauce. The sauce makes itself!

    1½ cups granulated sugar
    ⅓ cup all-purpose flour
    ¼ cup potato flour
    ½ tsp. salt
    1½ tbsp. grated lemon rind
    ⅓ cup lemon juice
    3 egg yolks, beaten
    3 tsp. soft butter or margarine
    1½ cups milk
    3 egg whites

Preheat oven to 350 degrees. Combine sugar, flour, potato flour, and salt. Stir in lemon rind, lemon juice, egg yolks, butter, and milk. Fold in stiffly beaten egg whites. Pour into a buttered 2-quart casserole. Set in a pan of hot water in oven. Bake 45 to 50 minutes. Serves 6.

ORANGE POTATO PUDDING (WITH VANILLA SAUCE)

4 egg yolks
⅓ cup granulated sugar
⅓ cup ground blanched almonds
2 tbsp. orange juice
1 tbsp. grated orange rind
1 cup mashed potato
4 egg whites

Preheat oven to 350 degrees. Beat egg yolks and sugar until thick and lemon-colored. Add almonds, orange juice, and rind. Beat in mashed potato. Whip egg whites until stiff and fold into potato mixture. Pour into a mold that has been lined with waxed paper. Place in a pan of hot water. Bake 45 minutes. Remove and cool 5 minutes. Unmold on serving platter. Serve with Vanilla Sauce. Serves 6.

VANILLA SAUCE

½ pkg (3¾-oz.) vanilla pudding
1 cup milk
1 egg yolk
2 tbsp. orange juice
1 tbsp. grated orange rind
1 tsp. rum flavoring (optional)

Combine pudding with milk and egg yolk. Cook over medium heat, stirring constantly until it thickens and begins to bubble. Add remaining ingredients. Stir. Pour over warm pudding.

APPLE-AND-POTATO COTTAGE PUDDING

The German people were the first to combine apples with potatoes. They called potatoes "earth apples," much as the French called them "pommes de terre" . . . apples of the earth.

6 medium tart apples, peeled and sliced
3 tbsp. brown sugar
3 tbsp. melted butter or margarine
1½ cups all-purpose flour
½ cup mashed potato
1½ tsp. baking powder
½ tsp. salt
¼ cup shortening
¾ cup granulated sugar
1 egg
¾ cup milk
1 tbsp. granulated sugar
1 tsp. cinnamon

Preheat oven to 350 degrees. Grease a 9" square cake pan. Combine apples, brown sugar, and melted butter. Spread in prepared cake pan. Combine flour, potato, baking powder, and salt. Cream shortening and sugar; add egg and beat well. Gradually add flour mixture alternately with milk. Pour over apples. Sprinkle with a mixture of cinnamon and sugar. Bake 45 minutes. Serve with whipped cream. Serves 6.

OHIO POTATO PUDDING

This is a nineteenth-century potato and carrot pudding served with Brown Sugar Rum Sauce (see Potato Christmas Pudding).

1 cup grated raw potato
1 cup grated raw carrot
1 cup currants
1 cup raisins
1 cup sugar (granulated or brown)
1 cup all-purpose flour
2 tsp. baking soda
1 tsp. salt

Combine vegetables and fruit. Thoroughly mix all other ingredients. Combine 2 mixtures and blend thoroughly. Place in a large pudding mold. Cover pudding bowl with tin foil. Place on a rack in a large cooking pot; add boiling water, 1 to 2" deep. Cover pot; steam 3 hours, adding water if needed. Cool 10 minutes; unmold. Serve warm with Brown Sugar Rum Sauce or any desired pudding sauce. Serves 8.

CANDY

Contrary to popular belief, many candies can be made at home without using special equipment. Over the years candy-making has become associated with special occasions. At our house we have good old-fashioned candy-making sessions at Christmas and Easter. The best and most special occasions, though, are the unexpected ones. When the wind howls and snow swirls around until you cannot see the house next door, it's time to make candy. This practice has gone on for over a quarter-century. Snowtime is candy time—candy sweetens the gloomiest day. And by using potatoes we add nutrition to a favorite treat.

Note: Icing sugar measurements for candy recipes are approximate as the amount required will vary according to the type (and wetness) of potato used.

THE POTATO COOKBOOK

POLISH POTATO BONBONS

¾ **cup warm mashed potato**
4 cups icing sugar
4 cups flaked coconut
1½ cups semi-sweet chocolate chips
1 square bittersweet chocolate
2 oz. (½ cake) paraffin wax

Blend together the mashed potato, sugar, and coconut. Form into balls the size of a small walnut. Melt chocolate and paraffin in a double boiler. Dip the potato balls into the chocolate mixture. Drain on waxed paper and let cool until firm.

Note: Variation: In place of chocolate, bits of cherry, lemon, or caramel can be used.

POTATO-PEPPERMINT PINWHEELS

These are a favorite at our house at Christmas.

½ cup mashed potato
1 tsp. vegetable oil
1 tsp. peppermint extract
Pinch of salt
5 cups sifted icing sugar
Few drops of red or green food coloring

Combine mashed potato, vegetable oil, peppermint extract, and salt. Beat well. Gradually add icing sugar to form a stiff dough. Divide into 2 dishes. Put a few drops of red or green food coloring in one dish. Knead both portions well. Roll as thinly as possible on plastic wrap. Place the white portion over the colored one and press together firmly. Roll tightly as for jelly roll. Wrap in plastic wrap and chill at least 2 hours. Cut in ¼" slices. Set on cookie sheet or waxed paper to dry for several hours. Store at room temperature in an airtight container.

CHOCOLATE CRUNCH CANDY

1 cup crunchy peanut butter
2 tbsp. butter or margarine
½ cup mashed potato
½ tsp. salt
1 cup coconut
1 cup Rice Krispies
2 cups icing sugar

Cream peanut butter, butter, and mashed potato. Add salt, coconut, Rice Krispies, and icing sugar. Mix well. Form into small balls.

CHOCOLATE DIP

8 oz. chocolate chips
½ bar paraffin wax

Melt chocolate chips and paraffin over hot water. Dip candy in chocolate mixture and cool on waxed paper. Store in refrigerator.

IRISH POTATO CANDY

½ cup cold mashed potato
¼ tsp. salt
½ tsp. vanilla
4 cups icing sugar (approximately)
1 cup peanut butter

Combine mashed potato, salt, and vanilla. Add enough icing sugar to make the mixture leave the sides of the bowl. Knead on a pastry board, using extra icing sugar as necessary. Divide dough and roll in 2 rectangles. Spread ½ cup peanut butter on each rectangle. Roll in jelly roll fashion. Wrap in waxed paper and refrigerate at least 2 hours. To serve, slice in thin slices.

POTATO CHOCOLATES

These chocolates can be made in a variety of flavors.

1 cup riced potato
1 tbsp. butter or margarine
1 tsp. flavoring of your choice
5 to 5½ cups icing sugar

Combine riced potato and butter. Beat with electric mixer or wooden spoon until light. Add flavoring and gradually work in icing sugar. Mixture should be a smooth firm dough. (I often mix in sugar before flavoring and then divide mixture into several small bowls. I then use a variety of flavorings and put a few drops in each dish. I sometimes use different food colorings to match the flavors.) Knead dough on a board. Form into small balls or shapes. Bits of nuts or cherries may be added.

CHOCOLATE DIP

4 oz. semisweet chocolate*
1" square paraffin wax
2 tbsp. butter or margarine
5 drops vanilla

Melt chocolate, wax, and butter in top of a double boiler. Stir until blended. Add vanilla. Heat mixture to 130 degrees then cool to 83 degrees. Keeping the temperatures between 83 degrees and 85 degrees, dip chocolates into mixture and coat thoroughly. Lift out carefully with 2 forks. Place on a rack covered with waxed paper. Draw a skewer across dipped candy to form a thread—the mark of an expert chocolate dipper. (If chocolate hardens, it can be melted, cooled to 83 degrees, and reused.)

*Use your choice of chocolate. I prefer semi-sweet or a mixture of 2 oz. semi-sweet and 2 oz. unsweetened.

AFTER-DINNER MINTS

1 medium potato, peeled and quartered
2 tbsp. milk
1 tsp. salt
1 tsp. vanilla
8 cups sifted icing sugar
Food coloring
Spearmint flavoring to taste (available in health food stores)

Boil potato in a small amount of water. When tender, remove cover and boil out all water. Beat until fluffy with an electric mixer. Add milk, salt, and vanilla. Slowly add sugar until mixture is very thick. Divide into 3 or 4 portions. Add desired food coloring and flavoring to each portion. Drop by teaspoons onto waxed paper or push through a cookie press. Let stand until firm. Store in an airtight container or freeze.

POTATO COCONUT FUDGE

1 cup hot mashed potato
Pinch of salt
2 tsp. soft butter or margarine
1 lb. icing sugar
1 tsp. vanilla
1 lb. coconut
2 oz. melted semi-sweet chocolate

Sprinkle salt over potato and spread with butter. Spoon into icing sugar and stir until very well-blended. Add vanilla and coconut. Put in a 9x12" cake pan. Dribble with melted chocolate.

Note: Variation: Use bitter chocolate or melted chocolate mint chips for a different taste.

CHOCOLATE-COVERED PEPPERMINT PATTIES

At our house it wouldn't be Christmas without Peppermint Patties!

1 cup mashed potato
6 to 8 cups icing sugar
1 tsp. salt
2 tbsp. melted butter or margarine
2 tsp. peppermint extract

Cream potato, sugar, salt, butter, and peppermint extract. Knead slightly. Form into balls the size of cherries. Flatten balls to firm circles. Let dry overnight at room temperature.

CHOCOLATE COATING

8 squares semi-sweet chocolate
½ bar paraffin wax

Melt semi-sweet chocolate and paraffin in top of a double boiler. Keep melted over hot water. (Do not heat too hot.) Dip patties in chocolate and let cool on waxed paper. In making candies, extra icing sugar may be needed, depending upon the dampness of the potatoes.

QUICK CHOCOLATE-POTATO FUDGE

3 squares chocolate (2 sweet and 1 unsweetened)
3 tbsp. butter or margarine
⅓ cup mashed potato
⅛ tsp. salt
1 tsp. vanilla
4 cups sifted icing sugar (approximate)

Melt chocolate and butter over hot water. Add the mashed potato, salt, and vanilla. Blend in sugar. Knead until smooth. Shape into a long roll about 1" in diameter. Cool and cut into slices.

Note: Variations: Try 3 ounces of semi-sweet chocolate chips instead of the squares. You can also use butterscotch, peanut butter, or chocolate mint.

STRAWBERRY SPUDS

½ cup mashed potato
1½ cups icing sugar
¼ tsp. salt
1 tbsp. soft butter or margarine
Strawberry gelatin

Combine potato, icing sugar, salt, and butter. Mix well. Form in strawberry shapes. Roll in gelatin powder. Garnish with green decorator's icing. Place a colored toothpick in the end of the "strawberry" for a stem.

Note: Variations: Form candy in various shapes and dust with different flavors of gelatin.

EASTER EGGS

For many years, these were the only Easter eggs to arrive at our house.

½ cup mashed potato
8 cups icing sugar
½ cup soft butter or margarine
Vanilla or peppermint flavoring (or your choice)
1 egg white
Chopped cherries, if desired
Chopped walnuts, if desired
Food colorings
1 pkg. (8-oz.) semi-sweet chocolate
1" square paraffin wax

Whip potato until very creamy. Add icing sugar, butter, and desired flavoring to taste. Blend in egg white and mix thoroughly. Set aside about ⅓ of mixture for "egg yolks." Add cherries or nuts to remaining mixture if desired. Blend thoroughly. To shape eggs, place a small amount of yellow mixture in center of each egg for a "yolk." Cover with other mixture. Form in egg shape approximately 1½" in diameter. Refrigerate until thoroughly cooled. Melt chocolate and paraffin over hot water in a double boiler. Dip chilled eggs in chocolate mixture to cover completely. Set on waxed paper to cool. When completely cooled these eggs can be decorated with children's names, flowers, etc. made from decorator's icing.

"Curiosity and interest are immediately aroused when you put into a young person's hands, a potato." *-Louis Pasteur*

PATSY'S POTATO BARS

Deliciously rich, the mixture is very stiff and must be pressed into the pan.

1 cup mashed potato at room temperature
8 cups sifted icing sugar
½ tsp. salt
½ cup soft butter or margarine
3 cups unsweetened coconut
2 tsp. vanilla
1 cup semi-sweet chocolate chips

Mix potato, icing sugar, salt, butter, coconut, and vanilla. Press firmly into a 9x13" cake pan. Drizzle with melted chocolate chips. Refrigerate. Cut in bars.

Note: Variation: Divide mixture into two 8" pans. Drizzle with melted butterscotch chips, peanut butter chips, or mint chocolate.

CHUNKY PEANUT-POTATO PINWHEELS

Do not make this recipe on a humid or wet day as candy will not firm properly.

⅓ cup cold mashed potato
¼ cup butter or margarine
1 tsp. vanilla
5 cups icing sugar
1 cup chunky peanut butter

Combine potato, butter, and vanilla. Blend well. Gradually add icing sugar. Knead. Roll between 2 sheets of waxed paper to about ½" thickness and the width of the waxed paper. Remove top sheet of waxed paper and spread peanut butter over the mixture. Roll up like a jelly roll. Leave wrapped in the waxed paper. Chill 2 to 3 hours. To serve, cut in small slices and serve at once.

POTATO FONDANT DAINTIES

These are colorful and delicious!

1 cup mashed potato
1 tbsp. butter or margarine
Flavoring and food coloring of your choice
5 to 5½ cups icing sugar

Combine all ingredients and knead well. Form into desired shapes and decorate. Refrigerate.

SHAPES AND FLAVORING IDEAS:

Banana: yellow food coloring, mini-banana shape
Strawberry: red food coloring, strawberry shape
Maple: top with walnut pieces
Almond: top with cherry bits
Mint: green food coloring

Note: Many of those beautiful cones of ice cream we see advertised on television are, in fact, fluffy mashed potatoes.

SALADS

Salads are no longer an eighteenth-century sun-season picnic dish. Equally popular for last-minute meals or make-ahead dinners, salads are becoming a year-round favorite. Salads may be an appetizer or an accompaniment or a meal in itself.

Salads are usually made from cooked or raw vegetables served with dressings and combinations of meats, fish, poultry, and eggs. They can be plain or garnished.

No picnic, barbecue, or Sunday family gathering would be complete without potato salad. Every country has its own special recipe. Here you will find a selection of the potato salads I have tried. All were equally delicious.

Once salad dressing has been added to potato salad, keep the salad well-chilled or serve immediately. You risk food poisoning by holding potato salads at room temperature.

GREEN BEAN AND POTATO SALAD

This is a deliciously different potato salad.

3 lb. new potatoes
3 oz. white wine or 1 oz. white wine vinegar
¼ cup chicken broth
½ cup French Oil and Vinegar Dressing
¾ tsp. summer savory
¾ tsp. basil
1½ lb. fresh green beans, cut in 1" pieces
Salt and pepper to taste

Scrub potatoes. Steam in small amount of water until just tender. Cool slightly and cut in quarters. While still warm, combine with wine and chicken broth and let stand for 20 minutes. Drain off any remaining liquid. Add French dressing, savory, and basil, and toss lightly. Chill covered for at least 4 hours. Steam beans until just tender. Chill under running water, pat dry on paper towels, and refrigerate 4 hours. Add beans to potatoes; season with salt and pepper, and toss gently. Serves 10 to 12.

FRENCH OIL AND VINEGAR DRESSING

¾ cup vegetable oil
¼ cup vinegar
1 tbsp. sugar
½ tsp. salt
Pinch pepper

Combine in a glass jar, cover, and shake.

CURRIED POTATO SALAD

6 large potatoes
½ cup Italian Dressing
1 cup chopped onion
2 cups mayonnaise
1 tbsp. curry powder
½ tsp. salt
1 tbsp. chopped parsley

Boil, peel, and dice potatoes. Cool. Add remaining ingredients and toss lightly. Chill. Serves 6 to 8.

ITALIAN DRESSING

1 cup vegetable oil
⅓ cup vinegar
2 tbsp. lemon juice
2 tsp. sugar
½ tsp. garlic salt
½ tsp. dry mustard
½ tsp. oregano
Pinch of pepper

Combine in a glass jar. Cover and shake well. Store in refrigerator. Shake before using. Makes 1½ cups.

SAVORY POTATO SALAD

6 medium potatoes, cooked, peeled, and cubed
½ tsp. savory
¼ tsp. marjoram
¼ cup vegetable oil
¼ cup vinegar
Salt to taste
¼ tsp. pepper
½ cup minced onion
1 cup seeded and diced cucumber
⅓ cup mayonnaise
2 tbsp. prepared mustard
Cucumber, tomato, radish, and lettuce for garnish, if desired

Place potatoes in a large bowl. Combine savory, marjoram, oil, vinegar, salt, and pepper in a jar; shake well to blend. Pour over potatoes and let stand 1 hour. Add onion, cucumber, mayonnaise, and mustard. Stir gently until thoroughly mixed. Garnish as desired. Serves 6.

SLENDER P.E.I. POTATO SALAD

This light and refreshing salad has a touch of curry. It's a winning addition to your buffet table or a pleasant alternative to the more traditional potato salad. And it's low-calorie besides!

1 cup plain yogurt
2 tsp. prepared mustard
1 tsp. curry powder
2 cups cubed cooked potatoes
1 cup sliced and quartered cucumber
½ cup sliced celery
¼ cup chopped onion
1 tbsp. chopped chives
Salt and pepper to taste

In a large bowl, combine yogurt, mustard, and curry. Add remaining ingredients; toss to mix well. Refrigerate for a few hours to blend flavors. Garnish with parsley flakes and fresh tomato wedges. Makes 8 servings (½ cup), about 55 calories each.

SEAFARER'S SALAD

Being a fisherman's daughter, I couldn't make a collection of salads without this old favorite that features potato chips and sardines.

2 medium heads lettuce
¼ cup grated cheddar cheese
¼ cup parmesan cheese
1 egg (raw)
¾ cup French Dressing
2 (4-oz.) cans sardines, drained
3 cups slightly broken potato chips

Break lettuce in small chunks. Sprinkle with cheese. Combine egg and French Dressing. Add to lettuce and cheese. Toss thoroughly. Add sardines and potato chips. Toss again lightly. Serve at once. Serves 8.

FRENCH DRESSING

¾ cup vegetable oil
¼ cup lemon juice
½ cup honey
½ tsp. celery salt
½ tsp. salt
¼ tsp. paprika
¼ tsp. dry mustard
¼ tsp. pepper

Combine all ingredients in a glass jar. Cover and shake well. Store in refrigerator. Shake before using. Makes 1 cup.

PARTY POTATO SALAD

This is great for summer barbecues.

10 cups sliced cooked potato
¼ cup vegetable oil
½ cup wine vinegar
1 tsp. salt
⅛ tsp. pepper
1 tsp. chives
8 slices bacon, cooked until crisp, then crumbled
4 hard-cooked eggs, diced
1 cup sliced celery
¼ cup chopped onion
¼ cup chopped green pepper
½ cup sour cream
½ cup mayonnaise
2 unpeeled cucumbers, scored with a fork lengthwise and sliced thinly

Combine potatoes, vegetable oil, vinegar, salt, pepper, and chives. Mix and chill. Add remaining ingredients at serving time. Mix lightly. Serves 10 to 12.

SHRIMP-AND-POTATO SALAD

1 cup chopped cooked shrimp
3 tbsp. vinegar or juice from sweet pickled gherkins
2 cups diced cooked potato
1 cup cooked peas, fresh or frozen
½ cup diced apple
3 gherkins or sweet pickles, chopped
1 tsp. salt
¼ tsp. pepper
1 tbsp. prepared mustard
2 tbsp. finely chopped fresh parsley
½ cup mayonnaise

Pour vinegar over shrimp. Let stand 10 minutes. Drain, saving vinegar. Mix shrimp with remaining ingredients. Stir in vinegar. Mix well. Chill 1 hour in refrigerator. Serves 4.

SAUSAGE-AND-POTATO SALAD

6 to 8 medium potatoes, peeled, cooked, and cubed
8 sausages, cooked and cut in quarters
½ cup mayonnaise
⅓ cup sour cream
1 tbsp. vinegar
1 green onion, finely chopped
½ tsp. dry mustard
½ tsp. tarragon
½ tsp. salt
Pepper to taste

Place potatoes and sausages in a large bowl. Stir together remaining ingredients; pour over potatoes and sausages. Toss lightly. Serve with greens. Serves 6 to 8.

MEAT-AND-POTATO SALAD MOLD

This is a special make-ahead summer salad.

MEAT LAYER

2 cups finely ground cooked meat (ham, chicken, or luncheon meat)
3 tbsp. minced onion
⅔ cup mayonnaise
½ cup chili sauce
2 tsp. prepared mustard
¼ tsp. Tabasco sauce
¼ tsp. celery salt
1 envelope unflavored gelatin
½ cup cold water

Combine meat, onion, mayonnaise, chili sauce, mustard, Tabasco sauce, and celery salt. Soften gelatin in cold water; heat over hot water until dissolved. Blend into meat mixture. Turn into an 8-cup salad mold. Chill until almost firm, approximately 1 hour.

POTATO LAYER

3 cups diced cooked potato
1 cup finely chopped celery
¼ cup chopped onion
¼ cup chopped green pepper
⅔ cup mayonnaise
1 tbsp. vinegar
1 tsp. salt
⅛ tsp. pepper
1 envelope unflavored gelatin
½ cup cold water

Combine potato, celery, onion, green pepper, mayonnaise, vinegar, salt, and pepper. Soften gelatin in cold water. Dissolve over hot water. Blend into potato mixture. Spread over meat mixture. Chill until firm. Serves 8.

MOLDED POTATO SALAD

1 pkg. lemon gelatin
¾ cup boiling water
½ cup cider vinegar
½ medium green pepper, chopped
1 cup mayonnaise
2 cups cubed cooked potato
1 stick celery, diced
1 tbsp. chopped red pepper
2 hard-cooked eggs, chopped
Salt and pepper to taste

Dissolve gelatin in boiling water and add vinegar. Chill until thick but not set. Beat in mayonnaise. Fold in remaining ingredients. Add salt and pepper. Pour into 1½-quart mold. Chill until set, approximately 1 hour. Unmold on bed of lettuce. Serves 6.

ITALIAN POTATO SALAD

1 cup diced cooked potato
1 cup diced and peeled apple
½ cup diced pickled cucumber (sweet or dill)
¾ cup chopped cooked carrot
¾ cup diced cooked meat (chicken or pork)
1 onion, chopped finely
1 tsp. chopped parsley
3 tbsp. vegetable oil
1 to 2 tbsp. vinegar
Salt and pepper to taste
Mayonnaise or yogurt to blend

Mix potato, apple, cucumber, carrot, meat, onion, and parsley. Add oil, vinegar, salt, and pepper. Let stand at least 1 hour. Mix with mayonnaise or yogurt to blend together. Makes 4 servings.

HAM'N'EGGS POTATO SALAD

8 medium potatoes, cooked, peeled, and cut in ½" cubes
2 tbsp. white wine vinegar
1¼ cups mayonnaise
1 tbsp. chopped dill
½ tsp. dry mustard
Pepper to taste
3 cups cooked ham, cut in ½" cubes
4 hard-cooked eggs, chopped
1 medium onion, finely chopped
Green pepper rings for garnish

While potatoes are still warm, sprinkle with vinegar. Blend mayonnaise, dill, mustard, and pepper in large bowl. Add potatoes, mix well, and let stand at room temperature for 15 minutes. Stir in ham, eggs, and onion. Refrigerate until serving time. Garnish with green pepper rings. Makes 8 servings.

GERMAN HOT POTATO SALAD

6 cups diced cooked potato
6 slices bacon, cut in small pieces
1 tbsp. all-purpose flour
1 tbsp. sugar
1 tsp. salt
½ tsp. dry mustard
⅛ tsp. pepper
⅛ tsp. paprika
¼ cup water
½ cup vinegar
⅛ tsp. celery salt
¼ cup finely chopped onion
¼ cup chopped celery
¼ cup chopped sweet pickle
2 hard-cooked eggs, chopped

THE POTATO COOKBOOK

Keep potatoes hot. Fry bacon until crisp; remove from pan. Combine flour, sugar, salt, mustard, pepper, and paprika and stir into bacon fat. Combine water and vinegar, and gradually add to mixture. Cook until smooth and thickened (about 5 minutes), stirring constantly. Pour over hot potatoes; add remaining ingredients and bacon, and toss lightly until well-mixed. Makes 6 servings.

GERMAN-STYLE CHILLED POTATO SALAD

Unlike the usual hot potato salads from Germany, this one is chilled well before serving.

5 lb. potatoes, boiled, peeled, and sliced
6 slices bacon, diced
½ cup all-purpose flour
4 cups water
6 tbsp. granulated sugar
1 tsp. salt
⅛ tsp. pepper
1 tsp. celery salt
¾ cup white vinegar
½ cup chopped onion
6 hard-cooked eggs, sliced

Place cold sliced potatoes in a large bowl. Fry bacon until crisp. Drain, reserving fat. Stir flour into bacon fat and blend well. Gradually add water, stirring constantly until thick. Add sugar, salt, pepper, and celery salt. Simmer until thoroughly blended. Add vinegar and bring to a boil. Pour over sliced potatoes; add onion and sliced eggs. Refrigerate to chill through. Serves 12 to 14.

DUTCH POTATO SALAD

1 cup diced cooked beef
1 dill pickle, minced
1 large apple, peeled and diced
1 cup diced cooked potato
1 small onion, minced
1 tbsp. vegetable oil
1½ tbsp. vinegar
2 tbsp. mayonnaise
2 hard-cooked eggs, sliced,
and shredded pickled beets for garnish

Combine beef, pickle, apple, potatoes, and onion. Mix together oil, vinegar, and mayonnaise; add to meat and potato mixture. Mix well. Put in bowl and garnish with hard-cooked egg slices and pickled beets. Serves 4.

Note: Raw potatoes are said to cure warts. I recently asked an elderly lady if this remedy worked. She assured me it did . . . if you used a stolen potato and were sure to bury it after application.

DANISH POTATO SALAD

Denmark is one of the many countries that combine potatoes with apples. Served with cold baked ham, this salad makes a meal to remember.

¼ cup oil
¼ cup vinegar
1½ cups diced apple
1½ cups diced cooked potato
1 cup diced cooked carrot
1 cup cooked peas (fresh, frozen, or canned)
4 hard-boiled eggs, chopped
½ cup chopped onion
½ cup mayonnaise
½ tsp. salt
⅛ tsp. pepper
Radish, celery, and/or green pepper, for garnish if desired

Mix oil and vinegar for dressing; combine apple and dressing. Mix well. Add potatoes, carrots, peas, eggs, and onion. Mix, then chill for 1 hour. Drain and add mayonnaise. Blend well, adding salt and pepper to taste. Put in bowl and garnish with raw vegetables if desired. Serves 4.

Note: The first potato recipes were in a book published in Germany in 1581 called *Ein New Kockbuch.*

POLISH POTATO SALAD

6 large potatoes, cooked, peeled, and diced
½ cup mayonnaise
½ cup cooked peas
½ cup diced cooked carrots
2 apples, peeled, cored, and diced
2 stalks celery, diced
2 dill pickles, chopped finely
1 tbsp. freshly chopped parsley
1 tbsp. chopped dill
½ cup sour cream
3 tbsp. vinegar
1 tsp. salt

Mix potatoes with mayonnaise and stand in refrigerator until well-chilled. Combine with remaining ingredients. Mix carefully and chill again before serving. Makes 6 to 8 servings.

HERRING, BEET, AND POTATO SALAD

This salad from Finland is really delicious.

6 medium potatoes, cooked and diced
6 beets, cooked and diced (about 2 cups)
2 apples, peeled and chopped
¼ cup finely chopped onion
1 cup diced pickled herring
½ tsp. salt
⅛ tsp. pepper
1 cup sour cream
¼ cup mayonnaise
2 to 3 tbsp. sugar
1 to 2 tbsp. vinegar

Combine potatoes, beets, apples, onion, and herring. Sprinkle with salt and pepper. Combine sour cream, mayonnaise, sugar, and vinegar. Stir into first mixture. Refrigerate 1½ to 2 hours before serving. Serves 6.

CARNIVAL POTATO SALAD

A colorful salad from the United States, this is sometimes called "Salmagundi."

2 cups diced cooked potato
2 cups diced cooked ham
½ cup chopped celery
½ cup cooked peas
2 hard-cooked eggs, chopped
1 tbsp. chopped pimento
2 chopped gherkins
½ to ¾ cup mayonnaise
½ tsp. salt
¼ tsp. pepper
Lettuce, radish, and 1 hard-boiled egg, for garnish, if desired

Combine potatoes, ham, celery, peas, eggs, pimento, gherkins, mayonnaise, salt, and pepper. Mix well. Put in a lettuce-lined bowl. Garnish with slices of hard-cooked egg and radish roses. Serves 4.

COTTAGE CHEESE POTATO SALAD

1 cup cottage cheese
4 cups diced cooked potato
3 tbsp. chopped sweet pickle
⅓ cup chopped green onion
½ cup chopped celery
¼ cup chopped green pepper
2 hard-cooked eggs, chopped
1 tsp. salt
¼ tsp. pepper
1 tsp. dry mustard
⅓ to ½ cup mayonnaise or salad dressing

Combine cheese, potatoes, pickle, green onion, celery, green pepper, and eggs. Mix together mustard, seasonings, and mayonnaise. Pour over salad and toss lightly. Chill thoroughly before serving. Makes 6 to 8 servings

SOUPS, STEWS, AND CHOWDERS

Soup can be an appetizer or a main course. It can be served hot or cold and it goes well with everything. How about soup and a sandwich, soup and salad, soup for dinner, or soup for lunch? Any time is soup time.

Soup begins with a good stock. The early settlers had a stock pot on the back of the stove. Each day, soup bones and bits of less-tender meats would go into the stock pot. Small amounts of vegetables and seasonings were added and when the dish had simmered until all the flavor was extracted from the various ingredients, the stock was strained and ready for the next day's soup.

Today we have it much easier, with commercial bouillon cubes and powdered soup bases. For those concerned about MSG in commercial bouillon cubes and powdered soup bases, some health food stores carry varieties without added MSG. However, whenever possible, I recommend making stock from leftover chicken and turkey, beef ribs and ham. I do occasionally use commercial products to enhance the flavors and I have used them in testing the recipes in this book.

Soups are easy to prepare, nutritious, and economical. There's a soup for every occasion, ranging from a clear broth to a chunky chowder.

Potatoes act as carriers and blend well with other ingredients, taking on the color and absorbing the flavor of whatever they are cooked with.

Most soups and stocks freeze well and actually improve in flavor if made a day early and reheated at serving time.

Potato soup is said to have originated with an American scientist, Benjamin Thompson, in 1795. He wanted to feed the poor, "as well as possible with as little as possible." Potatoes have been used in soup ever since.

THE POTATO COOKBOOK

CREAM OF POTATO SOUP

6 medium potatoes, peeled
6 cups water
1 tsp. salt
4 slices back bacon
3 medium onions
1 chicken bouillon cube
2 tbsp. soft butter
3 tbsp. all-purpose flour
2 cups milk

Combine potatoes, water, and salt. Cook until potatoes are tender. Cook and crumble bacon. Stir fry onion in bacon fat. Add bacon, bouillon cube, and butter to soup. Mash well or purée in a blender. Return to heat; mix flour and milk and add to soup. Heat through, but do not boil. Serves 6.

ACADIAN PEA SOUP

1 ham bone, with about 2 cups of meat left on
1½ cups dried yellow peas
3 cups diced raw potatoes
1 medium onion, diced
Pinch each of thyme, basil, and oregano
Salt and pepper to taste
1 tbsp. parsley flakes

Rinse peas. Place ham bone and peas in a 4-quart soup pot. Add enough cold water to cover ham bone (6 to 8 cups); bring to a boil. Skim off foam. Add potatoes, onion, and seasonings. Simmer 3 hours until peas are tender. Sprinkle with parsley. Remove bone from soup. Cut off meat and chop into small pieces. Return meat to soup, heat and serve. Serves 6 to 8.

VICHYSOISSE

A creamy potato soup that is equally good served hot or cold, this recipe comes from the P.E.I. Potato Marketing Board.

3 tbsp. butter or margarine
4 leeks, finely chopped
1 medium onion, chopped
1 quart chicken stock (may be made with bouillon base)
2 stalks celery, sliced
2 sprigs fresh chopped parsley
2 medium potatoes, peeled and sliced thinly
Salt to taste
½ tsp. pepper
Few drops Worcestershire sauce
Pinch curry powder
1 cup heavy cream
2 tbsp. chopped chives

Melt butter and add leeks and onion. Cook slowly until vegetables are tender but not brown. Add chicken stock, celery, parsley, potatoes, and seasonings. Cook mixture until potatoes are tender. Put soup through a fine sieve or purée in a blender at moderate speed until very smooth. Just before serving, stir 1 cup heavy cream into soup and simmer until heated. Serve hot, or chill and serve ice-cold. Sprinkle with finely chopped chives. Serves 4 to 6.

Note: Playwright Charles MacArthur taught his daughter Mary what to do when "a person at the dinner table becomes too stuffy": lob a wad of mashed potatoes off the back of a spoon at the victim. He demonstrated the technique on the governess, who was sitting across from him.

MOM'S MINESTRONE

A recipe from my mother's huge collection, this easy-to-prepare minestrone is extra special.

1½ lb. ground beef
2 cups diced potato
1 cup diced onion
1 cup zucchini
1 cup carrot
1 cup cabbage
½ cup celery
½ cup macaroni
½ cup canned tomato
7 cups water
1 bay leaf
½ tsp. thyme
Salt to taste
½ tsp. pepper
1 tsp. Worcestershire sauce
¼ cup parmesan cheese (optional)

Brown meat loosely in fry pan. Add remaining ingredients except for parmesan cheese. Bring to a boil. Lower heat and simmer for 1 to 1½ hours. Sprinkle with parmesan cheese to serve. Serves 6 to 8.

COCKALEEKIE (COCK-A-LEEK-E) SOUP

A famous dish from Scotland, this thick soup is served as a main course and eaten with a spoon and fork.

1 boiling fowl or broiler (3 to 3½ lb.) cut in large pieces
½ cup barley
4 cups boiling water
½ cup chopped carrot
½ cup chopped celery
¼ cup chopped onion
Salt to taste
¼ tsp. white pepper
1 bay leaf
Few sprigs fresh chopped parsley
1½ cups thinly sliced leek
½ tsp. thyme
1 cup peeled and cubed potato
2 cups milk or light cream

Place the cut-up chicken and barley in a large saucepan and cover with boiling water. Add carrot, celery, onion, salt, pepper, bay leaf, and parsley. Cover and let simmer until meat is ready to fall off the bones (1 to 2 hours, depending on the age of the bird). Remove chicken from saucepan and cool until easily handled. Discard bone and skin and chop meat into bite-sized pieces. Skim excess fat from the broth. Add leeks, thyme, and potato. Bring to a boil. Reduce heat; cover and simmer for 20 minutes or until barley and potato are tender. Add milk and cut-up chicken. Heat through. Remove and discard bay leaf before serving. Serves 8.

MEATLESS CABBAGE-AND-POTATO SOUP

Until researching this book I had never considered combining cabbage and potato in a soup almost "all-their-own." I was surprised to find Cabbage-and-Potato Soup is served in several countries, including Ireland and Russia. This recipe is easy to prepare and is very tasty.

3 cups boiling water
4 to 5 chicken bouillon cubes
3 medium potatoes, pared and diced
2 cups shredded cabbage
2 tbsp. margarine or butter
1 cup chopped leek or green onion
3 tbsp. all-purpose flour
1½ cups milk
2 tsp. prepared mustard
½ tsp. Worcestershire sauce
¼ tsp. pepper
¼ tsp. salt
2 drops Tabasco sauce
1½ cups cereal cream

Combine boiling water, bouillon cubes, potatoes, and cabbage. Cover and simmer over medium heat until potatoes are tender, about 10 minutes. Sauté leek in melted butter until tender. Stir in flour and cook 2 to 3 minutes. Slowly stir in milk. Add mustard, Worcestershire sauce, pepper, salt, and Tabasco sauce. Mix well and stir into broth and vegetable mixture. Slowly stir in cream. Cook over low heat for 15 minutes. Do not boil. Serves 6 to 8.

PUMPKIN-AND-POTATO SOUP

Pumpkin and potato soups are popular in many countries. A friend in Australia sent me several recipes for pumpkin soups. This one is my favorite.

¼ cup butter or margarine
1 medium onion, finely chopped
2 leeks or green onion, chopped
2 medium potatoes, peeled and diced
2 cups cooked pumpkin (canned pumpkin may be used)
2 cups boiling water
2 tbsp. chicken bouillon base
Salt and pepper to taste
2 cups milk or cream (I use half of each)
Chopped fresh parsley or chives for garnish

Sauté onion and leeks in butter until limp, but not brown. Combine with potatoes, pumpkin, water, and soup base. Simmer until potatoes are tender. Sieve or put through a blender. Stir in seasonings, milk, and cream. Heat slowly. Do not boil. Sprinkle with chives or parsley. Serves 4 to 6.

CORN CHOWDER

4 slices bacon, cut in small pieces
½ cup chopped onion
2 cups diced potato
1 cup boiling water
Salt to taste
⅛ tsp. pepper
1 tbsp. all-purpose flour
2 cups 2 percent evaporated milk
1 can (19-oz.) cream-style corn

Fry bacon until crisp; remove from pan and drain. Sauté onion in bacon fat. Drain off excess fat. Add potatoes, water, and seasonings. Cover and simmer about 10 minutes. Combine flour and milk. Add the vegetables. Stir until smooth and thick. Add corn and heat through. Sprinkle with bacon just before serving. Serves 4.

MULLIGAN STEW AND DUMPLINGS

⅓ cup margarine or butter
⅓ cup all-purpose flour
6 beef bouillon cubes
4 cups boiling water
2 cups diced cooked beef
4 medium onions, sliced
2 large carrots, diced
3 potatoes, diced
½ cup green beans
½ cup fresh or frozen peas
Salt and pepper to taste
Dash nutmeg

Melt margarine; stir in flour. Dissolve beef cubes in boiling water. Gradually stir into flour and margarine. Cook until it starts to thicken. Add beef, onions, carrots, potatoes, green beans. Bring to a boil and simmer for 30 minutes. Add peas, dumplings, and seasonings. Simmer, covered, 15 minutes longer. Serves 4 to 6.

DUMPLINGS

1 cup all-purpose flour
2 tsp. baking powder
2 tbsp. margarine, butter, or shortening
⅔ cup milk

Mix all ingredients and drop by spoonfuls into hot stew.

OVEN MEATBALL STEW

1 lb. ground beef
2 tbsp. onion
2 tbsp. green pepper
¼ cup cornmeal
1 tsp. salt
1½ tsp. dry mustard
1 tsp. chili powder
1 egg, slightly beaten
½ cup milk
¼ cup all purpose flour
2 tbsp. fat
2 cups tomato juice
4 medium potatoes, cut in large chunks
4 carrots, cut in large pieces
3 medium onions, quartered
Salt to taste

Combine ground beef, onion, green pepper, cornmeal, salt, mustard, chili powder, egg, and milk. Form into small meatballs. Sprinkle with flour and brown in hot fat. Place in a large casserole. Add remaining flour to frying pan. Blend in tomato juice. Cook until thick. Pour over the meatballs. Arrange vegetables around meat. Add salt to taste. Cover tightly. Bake at 350 degrees for 1 hour or until vegetables are tender. Serves 4 to 6.

SPICY CHUCKWAGON STEW

A spicy stew with thick chunks of vegetables and beef, this recipe comes from Texas.

2 lb. boneless beef, cut in 1" cubes
½ cup all-purpose flour
2½ tsp. salt
½ tsp. pepper
½ tsp. paprika
2 tbsp. vegetable oil
1 cup coarsely chopped onion
6 cups water
1 can (20-oz.) tomatoes
2 cups thickly sliced carrot
1 cup thickly sliced celery
3 cups potato, cut in 1" cubes
1 cup green peas
1 tsp. granulated sugar
3 tbsp. cornstarch
¼ cup cold water
Additional salt and pepper to taste

Coat beef cubes in mixture of flour, salt, pepper, and paprika, and brown in vegetable oil. Add onion and brown lightly. Add water, cover, and simmer for 30 minutes. Add vegetables and seasonings. Simmer uncovered for 30 minutes or until vegetables are tender. Blend some gravy from the stew into the cornstarch and water mixture and stir into stew until thickened. Serves 8 to 10.

AFTER-CLASS STEW

After a year of hamburgers, canned beans, and pizza, our son Mark decided his college cooking would have to improve. When packing his "care package" from home, I enclosed a frozen steak. With 1 pound of steak, he came up with a recipe to serve 6 college kids.

1 lb. flank steak, cut in thin strips
6 medium potatoes, sliced
3 medium carrots, diagonally sliced (to cook faster)
3 stalks celery, sliced
3 medium onions, sliced
1 cup cubed turnip
2 tbsp. oil
¼ tsp. garlic salt
3 heaping tsp. beef bouillon powder
Salt to taste
¼ tsp. pepper
1 tbsp. soy sauce
1 tsp. Worcestershire sauce
3 drops Tabasco sauce
1 can tomato soup
1 cup frozen peas
1 tbsp. water
1 tbsp. cornstarch

Cut steak and vegetables in thin diagonal slices. Sauté steak in oil until brown. Add all vegetables (except peas), seasonings, and soup. Simmer 30 minutes or until vegetables are tender. Stir in frozen peas. Combine cornstarch and water. Add to stew. Cook and stir until thickened and bubbly. Serve with hot biscuits. Serves 6.

P.E.I. CLAM CHOWDER

3 strips bacon, cut into 1" pieces
1 medium onion, chopped
2 tbsp. all-purpose flour
1 cup milk
1½ cups light cream
1 cup peeled and cubed potato
1½ cups clam juice
1 cup chopped cooked clams
1 tbsp. fresh chopped parsley, or 1 tsp. dry parsley

Fry bacon in a 2-quart saucepan over low heat until crisp. Remove and set aside. Reserve 1½ tbsp. bacon fat. Add onion to bacon fat and cook until transparent. Gradually stir in flour, blending well. Cook 1 minute. Slowly add milk and cream, stirring constantly until mixture is smooth and thick. Add bacon. Stir in potatoes and clam juice. Simmer until potatoes are tender, stirring often (about 15 minutes). Add clams. Simmer until thickened, stirring only to prevent sticking. Sprinkle with parsley. Serves 4.

LOBSTER CHOWDER

1 lb. lobster meat
2 tbsp. butter or margarine, melted
¾ cup thinly sliced onion
½ cup diced celery
2 cups diced potato
¾ cup diced carrot
3 cups boiling water
Salt to taste
⅛ tsp. pepper
1 cup evaporated milk

Cut lobster into bite-sized pieces; set aside. In a large saucepan, sauté onion and celery in butter until limp. Add potato, carrot, water, salt, and pepper. Bring to a boil. Add lobster and cook 10 to 15 minutes. Add milk. Heat, but do not boil. Serves 4.

Note: Variations: Any type of white fish may be used with this recipe. I have tried ling, cod, haddock, and canned chicken haddie. All are delicious.

ISLAND FISH CHOWDER

3 medium potatoes sliced in ¼" slices
½ cup diced celery
1½ lb. fish fillets
1 cup cold water
3 slices bacon
2 medium onions, sliced
1 cup boiling water
2½ cups milk
Salt to taste
¼ tsp. pepper
2 tbsp. butter
Fresh chopped parsley for garnish

Combine potatoes and celery. Cover with cold water and set aside. Cover fish with 1 cup cold water and heat to simmer for 5 minutes. Strain, reserving liquid. Cut fish in 2" pieces. Cut bacon into small pieces and fry in saucepan until crisp. Remove bacon; cook onion slices in bacon fat for 5 minutes. Drain potatoes and celery and add onion slices. Cover with boiling water. Simmer gently until potatoes are tender. Add fish and reserved fish liquid. Cover and simmer for 10 minutes. Add milk, salt, pepper, butter, and bacon. To serve, sprinkle with parsley. Serves 4.

SEAFOOD CHOWDER, MANHATTAN-STYLE

This main-course chowder can be kept 4 to 5 days in the refrigerator and it also freezes well. Reheating brings out even more flavor.

½ cup chopped bacon
2 medium onions, chopped
2 stalks celery, sliced thinly
3 to 4 medium potatoes, peeled and diced
1 can (28-oz.) tomatoes
3 tbsp. chicken soup base
3 cups boiling water
1 tbsp. chopped fresh parsley, or 1 tsp. dry parsley
1 tsp. thyme
salt to taste
½ tsp. pepper
1 lb. white fish, (e.g., cod, haddock, or ling)
½ lb. chopped scallops
1 can (7-oz.) shrimp

Sauté bacon. Crumble and set aside. Cook onions and celery in bacon drippings. Add potatoes and cook a few minutes. Add tomatoes, soup base, boiling water, parsley, thyme, and seasonings. Cook until potatoes are almost tender. Add white fish and simmer 10 minutes. Add scallops and shrimp and simmer another 6 to 8 minutes. Sprinkle with reserved bacon for garnish when ready to serve. Serves 6.

POPEYE'S FISH CHOWDER

You guessed it—this chowder features spinach along with fish and potatoes.

1 lb. fish fillets (any white fish)
½ cup salt pork or bacon, chopped
2 cups diced potatoes
2 stalks celery, chopped
3 tbsp. green sliced onion
2 tbsp. chicken soup base
2 cups boiling water
3 cups milk
3 tbsp. all-purpose flour
1 cup heavy cream
1 can (5 to 6-oz.) baby clams, undrained
2 cups finely shredded spinach
Salt to taste
¼ tsp. pepper
Dash of hot pepper sauce, optional

Chop fish coarsely. Cook pork or bacon in a Dutch oven until brown. Drain, reserving 3 tbsp. drippings. Add potatoes, celery, and onion to drippings. Cook until onion is tender. Add chicken soup base and water. Cover and cook 10 minutes or until potatoes are tender. Add fish and 2½ cups milk. Bring almost to a boil. Reduce heat; simmer until fish is cooked (3 to 5 minutes). Combine remaining cold milk and flour. Blend well. Stir into chowder. Cook and stir until bubbly. Cook 1 minute longer. Add cream, clams, spinach, salt pork, salt, pepper, and hot pepper sauce. Heat through but do not boil. Serves 8.

SALMON-VEGETABLE CHOWDER

One small can of salmon flavors this creamy chowder. Serve with crusty rolls for an economical lunch.

2 medium potatoes, cubed
1 cup water
1 cup milk
1 cup fresh or frozen mixed peas and carrots
1 tbsp. butter or margarine
2 tbsp. chopped onion
1½ tsp. all-purpose flour
1 can (7-oz.) salmon (remove bones and flake)
½ tsp. Worcestershire sauce
1 tsp. lemon juice
Salt to taste

Simmer potatoes in water and ¼ cup milk. Sauté onion in butter, stir in flour and add remaining milk to make a cream sauce. Add potatoes and bring close to a boil. Simmer 10 minutes. Add remaining ingredients. Heat but do not boil. Serves 2 to 4.

NEW ENGLAND TURKEY CHOWDER

¾ cup butter or margarine
2 cups diced celery
1 cup chopped onion
8 cups chicken or turkey broth (may be made with bouillon cubes)
2 cups diced cooked turkey
1 can (19-oz.) cream-style corn
4 cups cubed cooked potatoes
¾ cup cereal cream
1 tsp. ginger
Salt and pepper to taste

Sauté onion and celery in butter until transparent. Do not brown. Place broth in large covered kettle. Add remaining ingredients. Stir well. Heat thoroughly for 20 minutes, but do not boil. Season to taste. Serve in heated bowls with crusty rolls. Serves 8.

PARSNIP CHOWDER

So often parsnips are ignored. Here they combine with potatoes and onion for a delicious chowder.

2 tbsp. diced bacon
1 small onion, chopped
2 cups diced parsnips
1 cup diced potatoes
2 cups boiling water
Salt to taste
½ tsp. pepper
5 cups scalded milk
½ cup butter or margarine
½ cup finely crushed cornflakes
1 tbsp. fresh chopped parsley, or 1 tsp. dry parsley

Sauté bacon. Add onion and cook until tender. Add vegetables, seasonings, and water. Simmer until vegetables are tender. Stir in remaining ingredients and cook until chowder is almost to the boiling point. Do not boil after milk is added. Serves 6.

BAKED POTATOES

One of the most popular items in today's fast-food industry is the baked potato. Served with a variety of toppings, a baked potato is a quick nutritious snack, without an abundance of calories. In this section you will find a selection of easy-to-prepare potato toppings that you can make at home.

Another easy way to jazz up an old favorite is to stuff a baked potato. Included are several recipes for stuffings that will make baked potatoes a special treat.

Note: The Dutch potato industry is now worth more than the tulip industry. About ¼ of Dutch farmland is used for potatoes.

BAKED POTATOES

Select medium baking potatoes of uniform size. Scrub thoroughly with a vegetable brush. If desired, rub skins with oil to enhance flavor and appearance. Puncture skin in several places with a fork to prevent potatoes from exploding in the oven. Do not wrap in foil as this gives you soggy, steamed potatoes. Bake in hot oven (400 degrees) 45 to 60 minutes. After removing from oven, make a crosswise cut in each potato and pinch to let steam escape. If serving with the traditional butter, salt, and pepper, spread butter in the cuts on top of each potato and serve at once.

CLASSY BAKED POTATOES

Combining dairy foods with potato supplements the protein of the potato. Try 1 cup of the following dairy food bases:

Sour cream
Cottage cheese and lemon juice, blended
Mayonnaise
Yogurt OR
Cheese sauce seasoned with thyme, rosemary, paprika, or dry mustard

To this base add ¼ to ½ cup of one or a combination of the following ingredients:

Green onion	**Radish**
Chives	**Crisp bacon**
Fresh parsley	**Ham**
Celery	**Chicken**
Cucumber	**Sautéed mushrooms**

Makes enough for 4 to 6 potatoes.

SOUR CREAM AND CHIVES

1 cup sour cream
3 tbsp. minced chives
2 tbsp. minced parsley

Combine all ingredients and serve over hot baked potatoes. Serves 6.

MOCK SOUR CREAM

Cut calories with this delicious substitute.

½ cup water
1 tbsp. lemon juice
1 cup creamed cottage cheese
½ tsp. salt

Combine all ingredients in blender and purée at high speed until completely smooth (about 10 seconds), or beat with an electric mixer. Spoon onto hot baked potatoes as desired. Serves 6 to 8.

Note: Photos for stuffed baked potatoes are often taken with raw potatoes. Baked potatoes are tasty, but definitely not photogenic.

THE POTATO COOKBOOK

LOBSTER TOPPING

Dress up a baked potato with this creamy lobster topping.

1 cup canned diced lobster meat
1 pkg. (4-oz.) cream cheese
½ cup mayonnaise
¼ cup sour cream
2 tbsp. lobster juice
2 tsp. lemon juice
½ clove garlic, crushed
1 tsp. chives or parsley

Beat together cream cheese, mayonnaise, and sour cream. Add lobster juice, lemon juice, garlic, and chives. Beat well. Stir in lobster. Serve over hot baked potatoes. Serves 6 to 8.

YOGURT TOPPING

½ cup plain yogurt
1 to 2 tbsp. chopped sweet pickle
½ tsp. sugar
2 tbsp. chopped onion
Dash pepper
Dash celery salt
½ tsp. lemon juice

Combine all ingredients and chill. Serve on hot baked potatoes. Serves 4 to 6.

BACON-DILL TOPPING

4 slices bacon
¼ cup chopped dill pickle
¼ cup melted butter or margarine

Fry bacon until crisp. Drain on paper towels and crumble. Mix with pickle and butter. Serve over hot baked potatoes. Serves 6.

CHILI CHEDDAR TOPPER

1 medium chopped onion
¼ cup chopped green pepper
1 clove garlic, minced
2 tbsp. butter or margarine
1 lb. ground beef
1 tbsp. chili powder
¼ tsp. thyme
1 tsp. marjoram
1 can (15-oz.) tomato sauce
2 tbsp. ketchup
⅛ tsp. cayenne pepper
Shredded cheddar cheese

Sauté onion, green pepper, and garlic in butter for 5 minutes; add ground beef and cook another 5 minutes. Drain excess fat. Stir in chili powder, thyme, and marjoram; cook 3 minutes. Add tomato sauce, ketchup, and cayenne pepper seasoning. Cover and simmer until cooked through. Serve over baked potatoes; sprinkle with shredded cheddar cheese. Serves 6 to 8.

ITALIAN TOPPING

1 tsp. butter
2 tbsp. chopped onion
1 tbsp. chopped fresh parsley
¼ tsp. salt or celery salt
½ tsp. oregano
¼ tsp. basil
Dash pepper
1 cup diced tomato

Sauté onions in butter until transparent. Add remaining ingredients. Simmer 10 minutes. Keep warm until potatoes are cooked. Serves 4 to 6.

HAMBURGER STROGANOFF TOPPER

1 medium chopped onion
¼ lb. sliced mushrooms
2 tbsp. butter or margarine
¾ lb. hamburger
1 tsp. paprika
1 tsp. prepared mustard
½ cup beef broth
½ tsp. salt
¼ tsp. pepper
1¼ cups sour cream

Sauté onion and mushrooms in butter; add hamburger and cook until pinkness leaves meat. Drain excess fat. Stir in paprika, prepared mustard, beef broth, salt, and pepper. Simmer until well-blended. Just before serving, stir in sour cream and heat to serving temperature. Do not boil. Serve over hot baked potatoes. Serves 6 to 8.

CHINESE-STYLE BAKED POTATOES

1 lb. sliced mushrooms
½ cup sliced green pepper
½ cup chopped onion
1 clove garlic, minced
¼ cup vegetable oil
2 tomatoes, chopped
1 can (8-oz.) whole kernel corn, drained
1 tbsp. soy sauce
1 tbsp. vegetable oil
½ tsp. sugar
1 tsp. grated ginger root

Stir fry mushrooms, green pepper, onion, and garlic in oil until crispy-tender. Add tomatoes and corn, and stir fry 3 minutes longer. Add soy sauce, oil, sugar, and ginger root. Heat through. Cut baked potatoes almost in half, lengthwise; fluff with a fork and top with vegetable mixture. Serves 6.

STUFFED BAKED POTATOES

Bake medium-sized potatoes at 400 degrees 45 to 60 minutes. Cut potato open. Scoop out insides; mash. Add hot milk, butter, and seasonings. Beat until fluffy; pile lightly into potato shells, return to oven and brown.

SOME IDEAS FOR SEASONINGS
(Amounts are for 1 potato):

3 tbsp. grated cheese
1 tbsp. diced onion
¼ cup cooked meat with 1 tsp. diced onion
2 tbsp. crisp bacon bits
1 tsp. chopped chives or parsley flakes
¼ cup salmon with 2 tbsp. cooked peas

TWICE-BAKED CHEESE-STUFFED POTATOES

4 medium baked potatoes
1½ cups shredded Gouda cheese
½ cup sour cream
2 tbsp. butter or margarine
2 tbsp. finely chopped green onion
1 tbsp. fresh chopped parsley
1 tbsp. horseradish (optional)
¾ tsp. salt
4 slices bacon, cooked to crisp and crumbled

Cut baked potatoes in half, lengthwise. Scoop out center and mash with 1 cup cheese, sour cream, butter, onion, parsley, horseradish, and salt. Mix well. Fill potato shells with mixture; sprinkle with remaining cheese. Bake at 350 degrees for 20 minutes. Sprinkle bacon over potatoes for last few minutes of baking. Serves 4.

REUBEN SPUDS

¼ cup corned beef, cut in thin strips
½ cup drained sauerkraut
¼ cup shredded Swiss cheese

Preheat oven to 350 degrees. Split baked potato almost in half lengthwise. Fluff potato with fork. Top with corned beef, sauerkraut, and cheese. Bake until cheese melts, about 10 minutes. Serve with mustard if desired. Serves 1.

Note: The first toy advertised on American television is said to have been "Mr. Potato Head."

LOW-CALORIE STUFFED BAKED POTATOES

4 medium baked potatoes
⅔ cup skim milk
1 cup cottage cheese
Salt
Pepper
Paprika

Preheat oven to 400 degrees. Cut baked potatoes in half, lengthwise. Scoop out potato and mash well with milk, cottage cheese, and salt and pepper to taste. Spoon into potato shells; sprinkle with paprika and bake until lightly browned. Serves 8. Approximately 75 calories per serving.

CRAB-STUFFED BAKED POTATOES

Rock crabs are abundant in most fishing areas of Prince Edward Island. In recent years crab fishing has become an important industry. This delicious recipe using rock crab with potatoes comes from the P.E.I. Department of Fisheries.

6 baked potatoes
1 tbsp. softened butter or margarine
¾ cup sour cream
1 small onion, grated
¼ tsp. cayenne pepper
6 oz. fresh rock crab meat (cartilage removed)
¼ cup diced mushroom
½ cup grated cheddar cheese

Preheat oven to 375 degrees. Cut baked potatoes in half lengthwise and carefully scoop out insides, reserving the skins. In a medium bowl combine potato, butter, sour cream, onion, and cayenne pepper. Mash with a potato masher until smooth. Fold in crab meat and diced mushrooms. Spoon mixture into the 12 potato halves. Sprinkle with grated cheese and place on a baking sheet. Bake 10 to 15 minutes until hot. Serve at once. Serves 6.

LOBSTER-STUFFED BAKED POTATOES

Prince Edward Island lobster and potatoes makes a perfect combination.

½ cup diced cooked lobster meat
6 baked potatoes
1 tbsp. butter or margarine
½ cup sour cream
¼ cup grated onion
¼ tsp. pepper
¼ cup diced mushrooms
½ cup grated cheddar cheese

Preheat oven to 375 degrees. Cut baked potatoes in half lengthwise and carefully scoop out insides, reserving the skins. In a bowl, mash the potato, then add butter, sour cream, onion, and pepper. Beat until smooth. Fold in lobster meat and mushrooms, and place mixture back in the potato skin halves. Sprinkle with grated cheese and place on a baking sheet. Bake 15 to 20 minutes, or until potatoes are heated through. Serves 6.

SAUSAGE-STUFFED BAKED POTATOES

8 large baked potatoes
1 cup scalded light cream
⅓ cup melted butter or margarine
2 tsp. salt
¼ tsp. pepper
8 pork sausages, cooked
2 tsp. minced fresh parsley
½ tsp. Worcestershire sauce
Paprika

Preheat oven to 400 degrees. Cut tops of potatoes lengthwise. Scoop out pulp and mash with cream, butter, salt, and pepper until fluffy. Fill potato shells half-full with this mixture; put in a cooked sausage and sprinkle with parsley and a few drops of Worcestershire sauce. Cover with remaining potato mixture. Sprinkle with paprika and bake until heated through and brown on top (about 15 minutes). Serves 8.

SALMON-STUFFED BAKED POTATOES

The P.E.I. Department of Fisheries developed this recipe.

6 baked potatoes
½ cup hot milk
1 tsp. salt
¼ tsp. pepper
¼ tsp. thyme
1 egg, beaten
2 (7-oz.) cans pink salmon
¼ cup finely chopped onion
1 tbsp. parsley flakes
½ cup fine dry bread crumbs
¼ cup melted butter or margarine

Cut potatoes in half lengthwise while hot. Scoop insides of potatoes into a bowl, keeping shells intact. Set shells on a large baking pan. Add hot milk to potato and beat or mash until light and fluffy. Add salt, pepper, thyme, and egg, and blend well. Drain salmon and flake. Fold salmon, onion, and parsley into potato mixture. Spoon mixture into the potato shells. Combine bread crumbs and butter and sprinkle over potato. Bake at 400 degrees for about 20 minutes or until browned and heated through. Serves 6.

ACCOMPANIMENTS

Accompaniments are the "little extras" that demonstrate flair. Try potato pancakes for Sunday brunch or as a side dish with steak, roast, ham, or barbecued meats. How about some home fries for a country-style harvest-time breakfast? Crispy fries and creamy casseroles that mix well with other vegetables, as well as many exciting new ideas, are found in this section.

Note: Twenty pounds of potatoes can grow a ton of food in 1 year.
China in 1984 grew 12.5 million acres of potatoes.
Potatoes occupy approximately 50 billion acres of land worldwide.
The potato grows from below sea level in the Netherlands to altitudes of 14,000 feet in the Himalayas and Andes mountain regions.
Potatoes are grown in the deserts of Australia and Africa.
Potatoes have been grown on Ellesmere Island, north of the Arctic Circle.

QUICK POTATO ACCOMPANIMENTS

SAUSAGE POTATOES

Remove centers from baking potatoes with an apple corer. Insert part of a sausage into each potato. Bake in a cake pan, basting from time to time with the fat that drips from the sausage.

JULIENNE OR SHOESTRING POTATOES

Peel potatoes. Cut in thin strips (¼ x ¼ x 2"). Soak in ice water for 45 minutes. Drain. Dry between towels. Deep fry in fat at 325 degrees until brown. Drain on brown paper or paper towels.

HOME-MADE POTATO CHIPS

Peel potatoes. Slice thinly; cover with ice water and let stand for 45 minutes. Drain. Dry on towels. Deep fry in fat at 325 degrees until golden brown. Drain on brown paper. Sprinkle with salt.

POTATOES LYONNAISE

Potatoes Lyonnaise is a fancy name for fried potatoes. Simply sauté onion in fat, add diced cooked potatoes, and fry until browned on the bottom and well heated through. Sprinkle with salt and pepper.

POTATOES PERSILLADE (PARSLEY POTATOES)

Add ½ cup lemon juice to ½ cup melted butter or margarine. Pour over whole new cooked potatoes. Sprinkle with fresh chopped parsley.

FRENCH FRIED POTATOES

Cut peeled or unpeeled potatoes into sticks ¼ to ½" thick. Soak for 45 minutes in ice water. Drain and dry thoroughly. Deep fry in hot fat at 370 degrees for 5 to 7 minutes. Drain on absorbent paper. Sprinkle with salt. Do not put too many potatoes in the serving dish at once or French fries will become soggy.

ROAST POTATOES

Peel and quarter medium-sized potatoes. Parboil for 8 to 10 minutes. Put in a pan with a roast about 45 minutes before the meat is done. Baste with meat juices. Save the water from parboiling the potatoes to use in gravy or other recipes.

FLEMISH HASH

Rice or sieve hot boiled potatoes. To each cup of potatoes add ½ cup buttermilk, 1 tbsp. butter or margarine, and salt and pepper to taste. Beat thoroughly until light and fluffy. Serve with any meat or fish dinner.

QUICK CROQUETTES

Season leftover mashed potatoes with salt and pepper. Add 1 tsp. butter or margarine for each cup of potatoes. Form into patties. Coat with Shake 'N Bake, bread crumbs, crushed cornflakes, or flour and seasonings. Bake until crispy in a moderate oven (350 degrees) for 15 to 20 minutes.

HASH BROWNS

Today's "hash browns" were yesterday's ordinary fried potatoes—the only difference is the addition of a few onion slices. These were served almost nightly on P.E.I.

One of my best memories is the smell of fresh baked bread and fried potatoes when I arrived home from school.

2 tbsp. fat (butter or margarine, bacon drippings, or vegetable oil)
2 cups cubed cold boiled potato
1 tbsp. parsley flakes
½ tsp. salt
Dash pepper
Finely chopped onion

Melt fat in a heavy frying pan. Add other ingredients. Mix well, fry until browned. Serves 2.

BARBECUED POTATOES AND CARROTS

Enjoy barbecued flavor year-round with this oven-baked recipe.

4 cups thinly sliced potatoes, peeled or unpeeled
1 cup carrot, sliced diagonally to speed cooking
½ cup chopped celery
½ cup chopped onion
½ cup shredded cheese of your choice
3 tbsp. all-purpose flour
Salt and pepper to taste
⅓ cup ketchup
⅛ tsp. cayenne pepper
1 tsp. Worcestershire sauce
½ tsp. garlic salt
2 cups milk

Preheat oven to 375 degrees. Combine potatoes, carrots, celery, onion, and cheese. Add flour, salt, and pepper and mix well. Put in greased casserole. Combine remaining ingredients and pour over vegetable mixture. Cover and bake for 1 hour. Stir. Bake uncovered until cooked through and browned on top. Serves 4 to 6.

Note: On her way down to the local pond where my mother-in-law as a child went ice skating, she would carry baked potatoes in her skates. When she arrived at the pond, she had warm skates to wear. She put the same potatoes in her boots to ensure cozy feet on the long walk home.

POTATO KNISHES

Knishes originated in Israel. Popular now throughout many parts of the world, they were introduced to me by Cindy Chase of Halifax, Nova Scotia. This recipe was first published in Peru in the CIP Women's Club cookbook.

DOUGH

6 cups all-purpose flour
1 tsp. baking soda
1 egg
1 egg white
1½ cups lukewarm water
¾ cup vegetable oil

FILLING

12 medium potatoes (about 4 lb.), cooked and mashed
1½ cups chopped onion
¼ cup vegetable oil
2 beaten eggs
Salt and pepper to taste

DOUGH: Combine flour and soda. Make a hole in the center and add beaten egg and egg whites and ¼ cup of water. Gradually mix with a knife, working from the inside out and adding more water in small amounts (about ¼ cup at a time). When well-mixed, divide into 6 balls. Knead with your hands and throw dough on counter top several times. With a small amount of flour, add 1 tbsp. of oil to each roll. Knead until smooth and elastic enough for a thumb print to stay for a few seconds in the dough. Place dough in a pie plate and pour remaining oil over balls to soak. Let stand at least 1 hour before using.

FILLING: Sauté onions in vegetable oil. Mix potatoes with onions, eggs, salt, and pepper.

To assemble knishes, roll dough with a rolling pin; press with hands until very thin. Holding dough in your hands above a table, begin stretching in the middle and working toward the outside. Each ball of dough should be as thin as paper (about 1/16 of an inch). Form potato mixture into a long slender roll, about 1 inch in diameter. Roll dough around potato mixture. Seal. Preheat oven to 400 degrees. Cut rolls into 1½" pieces. Push ends partially shut and place ends down on a shallow greased baking sheet. Bake 45 minutes in a 400-degree oven, until lightly browned. Makes 12 knishes.

SCALLOPED POTATOES

6 medium potatoes, peeled and thinly sliced
1 medium onion, sliced
2 tbsp. all-purpose flour
1 tsp. salt
Pepper to taste
2 cups hot milk
2 tbsp. butter or margarine

Preheat oven to 350 degrees. Layer sliced potatoes and onion in casserole. Sprinkle flour, salt, and pepper over layers. Cover with hot milk and dot with butter. Bake 1 hour covered. Remove cover for last 15 minutes of cooking time. Serves 4 to 6.

Note: Gangster John Dillinger is reported to have carved a pistol from a potato. He dyed it with iodine, which facilitated his escape from prison.

CELERY-CHEESE POTATO SCALLOP

This can be made ahead and frozen. Thaw before reheating.

2 tbsp. onion
2 tbsp. celery leaves
Few sprigs fresh chopped parsley
1½ tbsp. all-purpose flour
2 tbsp. butter or margarine
¾ tsp. salt
⅛ tsp. pepper
¾ cup milk
3 medium potatoes, peeled and sliced
1 cup grated cheddar cheese
Dash paprika

Blend onion, celery, parsley, flour, butter, salt, pepper, and milk in a blender. Arrange potato slices in a buttered 1-quart casserole. Pour blended mixture over potatoes. Sprinkle with cheese and paprika. Bake at 350 degrees for 1 hour. Serves 4.

WHIPPED CREAM POTATOES

Serve with steak, fried chicken, or baked ham—these mashed potatoes are out of this world!

8 medium potatoes, boiled and mashed
1 tsp. salt
1 pint whipping cream
½ lb. grated cheddar cheese

Combine mashed potatoes and ½ pint of whipping cream. Beat at medium speed with electric mixer until thick and creamy. Add salt and pepper to taste and sprinkle with half the grated cheese. Stir lightly. Put in a large baking dish. Whip remaining ½ pint of cream. Spread over potato mixture. Sprinkle with remaining cheese. Bake uncovered at 300 degrees for 1 to 1½ hours. Serves 8 to 10.

SPINACH AND POTATO CASSEROLE

Double this recipe and freeze half for later. Swiss chard may be used instead of spinach.

4 to 5 medium potatoes, cooked and mashed
⅓ cup sour cream
1 tsp. salt
Dash pepper
½ tsp. granulated sugar
½ cup butter or margarine
¼ to ½ cup milk
2 tsp. chopped chives
⅛ tsp. dill seed
1 cup cooked well-drained spinach
½ cup grated cheddar cheese

Preheat oven to 400 degrees. Combine potatoes, sour cream, salt, pepper, sugar, and butter. Add enough milk to make a fluffy mixture. Stir in chives, dill seed, and chopped spinach. Put in a greased casserole. Sprinkle with cheese. Bake 20 minutes. Serves 4 to 6.

POTATO DUMPLINGS

6 medium potatoes, boiled and mashed well
1 tsp. salt
½ tsp. pepper
2 tbsp. melted shortening
1 tsp. nutmeg
4 eggs, beaten
2 tbsp. all-purpose flour
2 tbsp. bread crumbs

Combine all ingredients and beat thoroughly. Drop by spoonfuls into salted boiling water. Cover tightly and boil about 12 minutes. Yields 20 dumplings.

POTATO CHEESE DUMPLINGS

This recipe from Jamaica is served with sausages. Unlike most dumpling recipes, it is not boiled.

3 lb. potatoes, mashed (8 to 9 medium potatoes)
¼ cup butter
3 tbsp. milk
½ tsp. salt
¼ tsp. pepper
¾ cup grated cheddar cheese
Paprika

Preheat oven to 375 degrees. Combine potatoes, butter, milk, salt, and pepper. Form into balls. Roll in grated cheese. Bake in a well-buttered pan or casserole dish for about 20 minutes. Serves 8.

POTATO SOUFFLE

Soufflés are not as difficult to make as many believe. Surprise your guests with this light and tasty version.

3 cups hot mashed potato
2 tbsp. butter
2 tbsp. chopped onion
1 tsp. salt
2 tsp. chopped parsley
Shake of cayenne pepper (optional)
3 eggs, separated

Preheat oven to 350 degrees. Combine potato, butter, onion, salt, parsley, and cayenne pepper; mix thoroughly. Beat egg whites until stiff. Beat egg yolks and add to potato mixture. Gently fold in egg whites. Put in a greased soufflé dish. Set in a pan of water. Bake 1 hour. Serves 4.

POTATOES ALASKA

Also called "Snow-capped Potatoes," these tiny potato "mountains" are made with mashed potato.

4 medium potatoes, cooked and mashed
2 tbsp. butter or margarine
2 egg yolks
2 tbsp. chopped green onion tops or chives
½ tsp. salt
Dash pepper
2 egg whites
2 tbsp. mayonnaise
½ tsp. lemon juice

Preheat oven to 350 degrees. Combine potatoes, butter, egg yolks, green onion, salt, and pepper. Mix well. Using an ice cream scoop, make mounds of potatoes on a foil-covered baking sheet. Beat egg whites until stiff peaks form; fold in mayonnaise and lemon juice. Top each potato mound with a spoonful of egg-white mixture. Bake for 10 to 12 minutes. Serves 6 to 8.

SWISS-PARMESAN POTATO CASSEROLE

1¼ cups grated parmesan cheese
½ tsp. salt
⅛ tsp. pepper
¼ tsp. nutmeg
6 potatoes, peeled and thinly sliced
6 tbsp. butter
½ cup cream
½ cup grated Swiss cheese
2 tbsp. chopped chives

Preheat oven to 400 degrees. Mix together parmesan cheese, salt, pepper, and nutmeg. Layer potatoes in a buttered 2-quart casserole dish, sprinkling each layer with the cheese mixture. Dot with butter and cover tightly; bake for 1 hour. Uncover and pour cream over the top. Sprinkle with Swiss cheese. Bake uncovered for 5 minutes until cheese melts. Sprinkle with chives before serving. Serves 6.

DUCHESS POTATOES

Try this recipe at your next dinner party. Serve with a roast or with baked stuffed salmon.

> **3 cups hot riced potato**
> **2 tbsp. butter**
> **1 tsp. salt**
> **Few grains paprika**
> **3 egg yolks, beaten**
> **1 egg yolk, beaten with 1 tbsp. cold water**

Preheat oven to 350 degrees. Combine potato, butter, salt, paprika, and egg yolks. Use a pastry bag to form rosettes or pyramids in a baking dish. Brush with egg yolk-water mixture. Bake for 15 minutes.

Note: Variation: Duchess Potatoes make a nice topping for casseroles or meat loaf.

Note: Potatoes provide more edible matter than the combined worldwide consumption of milk, meat, poultry, and seafood.

CHICKEN CURRIED POTATOES

Chicken stock and a light taste of curry powder add an eastern taste to potatoes. Serve with roast chicken.

4 tbsp. butter
¼ cup finely chopped onion
3 cups cold cooked potato cubes
⅔ cup chicken stock (may be made with bouillon powder)
1 tsp. curry powder
1½ tsp. lemon juice
Salt and pepper to taste

Sauté onion in butter until limp. Do not brown. Add potatoes and cook until butter is absorbed. Add chicken stock and seasonings. Cook until liquid is absorbed into the mixture. Serves 4.

ROADSIDE POTATOES

I have often wondered where this recipe got its name!

1 large onion, cut in chunks
1½ tsp. all-purpose flour
2 tsp. salt
Few drops Tabasco sauce
1 cup milk
4 medium potatoes, peeled
1 cup grated cheddar cheese

Preheat oven to 350 degrees. Grease an 8" square cake pan. Put onion, flour, salt, Tabasco sauce, and milk in a blender. Purée until completely blended. Grate potatoes and cheese into milk mixture. Pour into prepared pan. Bake 1 hour or until cooked through and golden on top. Serves 4.

BASQUE POTATOES

This recipe can be prepared in an electric frying pan. It's nice for summer menus when you don't want to heat the kitchen by using the oven.

1 medium onion, sliced
1 clove garlic
2 tbsp. vegetable oil
¾ cup fresh chopped parsley
¼ cup pimento
⅛ tsp. pepper
1 chicken bouillon cube
1 cup hot water
6 to 8 medium potatoes, peeled and thinly sliced

Sauté onion and garlic in vegetable oil. Remove and discard garlic. Layer thinly sliced potatoes and onion in skillet. Combine other ingredients and pour over potatoes. Heat to boiling. Cover and simmer until potatoes are tender, about 20 minutes. Serves 6 to 8.

OOH-LA-LA POTATOES

This recipe from France is best if made a day ahead and reheated.

6 medium potatoes, cooked, peeled, and cubed
1 cup shredded cheddar cheese
6 tbsp. butter or margarine
¾ cup sour cream
3 green onions, chopped
1 tsp. salt
¼ tsp. pepper

Preheat oven to 300 degrees. Melt cheese and butter. Combine with remaining ingredients. Bake in a greased 2-quart casserole dish for 25 minutes. Serves 6.

POTATO PHILI

This casserole can be made ahead and frozen. Thaw before baking.

8 medium potatoes, cooked and mashed
4 oz. cream cheese
½ cup plain yogurt
1 tbsp. onion salt
⅛ tsp. pepper
1 tbsp. butter

Preheat oven to 350 degrees. Stir ingredients into mashed potatoes and put in a greased casserole dish. Dot with butter. Bake covered for 30 minutes. If freezing, cover tightly with plastic wrap. Cool in refrigerator and then place in freezer. Thaw before baking. Serves 8.

POTATOES HOLLANDAISE

3 cups sliced raw potato
Enough chicken broth to cover
⅓ cup butter or margarine
1 tbsp. lemon juice
Salt to taste
1½ tsp. finely chopped parsley

Cook potatoes in stock. Drain. Cream butter, lemon juice, and salt. Add to potatoes and cook 3 minutes. Sprinkle with parsley. (Discard chicken stock or use in soup or gravy.) Serves 4.

O'BRIEN POTATOES

Two cups diced cooked meat or fish may be added for a variation of this Irish recipe.

4½ cups diced cooked potato
1 cup chopped onion
½ cup chopped celery
¾ tsp. salt
Dash pepper
¼ cup fresh chopped parsley
¼ cup oil

Combine potato, onion, celery, salt, pepper, and parsley. Fry in fat until slightly browned and thoroughly heated. Serves 4 to 6.

SPANISH POTATOES

¼ cup butter or margarine
¼ cup chopped onion
2 tbsp. chopped green pepper
2 tbsp. chopped pimento
4 cups boiled potatoes (use small whole potatoes or diced potatoes)
Salt and pepper to taste

Sauté onion, pepper, and pimento in butter. Add drained potatoes and cook until brown. Season with salt and pepper. Serves 6.

CHANTILLY POTATOES

3 cups mashed potato
½ cup grated cheddar cheese
½ cup stiffly beaten heavy cream

Preheat oven to 325 degrees. Pile mashed potatoes in a baking dish. Spread cream over potatoes and sprinkle with cheese. Bake until delicately browned, 20 to 30 minutes. Serves 6.

POTATO APPLESAUCE BAKE

Don't let this applesauce surprise you! Many countries combine apples with potatoes. This recipe is delicious with pork chops or fried chicken.

4 cups mashed potato
3 tbsp. butter
3 tbsp. milk
½ tsp. salt
⅛ tsp. pepper
2 cups applesauce
¼ tsp. cinnamon
¼ cup diced onion
1 tbsp. parsley
1 tbsp. butter
Paprika

Preheat oven to 350 degrees. In a large bowl combine mashed potato with butter, milk, salt, and pepper. Beat well. Put a layer of this mixture in the bottom of a well-greased 1½-quart casserole. Mix cinnamon and applesauce. Spread half this mixture over the potatoes. Sprinkle with chopped onion, celery salt, and parsley. Drip butter over mixture. Repeat layers and end with a layer of potatoes on top. Sprinkle with paprika. Bake 25 to 30 minutes until heated through. Serves 4 to 6.

SUGAR-BROWNED POTATOES

This is an excellent recipe when made with Sebago potatoes, although any small, smooth, evenly formed potato works well.

1 lb. small potatoes
Salted water
2 tbsp. granulated sugar
¼ cup melted butter or margarine

Cook potatoes until just tender in salted water. Drain. Cool slightly. Combine sugar and butter in a skillet. Add potatoes and heat, stirring frequently until potatoes are evenly browned and glazed. Serves 4.

CHEDDAR-CHEESE SCALLOPED POTATOES

This easily prepared version of an old favorite can be made ahead, frozen, and reheated.

6 medium potatoes, peeled and sliced
¼ cup sliced onion
¼ cup chopped celery
3 tbsp. all-purpose flour
¼ cup butter
1½ tsp. salt
¼ tsp. pepper
1½ cups milk
1 cup grated cheddar cheese
Dash paprika

Preheat oven to 350 degrees. Arrange potato slices in a greased 2-quart casserole dish. Combine onion, celery, flour, butter, salt, and pepper in a blender. Pour in milk and blend for 30 seconds. Pour mixture over potato slices; sprinkle with cheese and paprika. Bake for 45 to 55 minutes. Serves 6 to 8.

DUTCH POTATO CASSEROLE

6 medium potatoes, boiled and sliced thinly
2 tbsp. chopped onion
1 tbsp. fresh chopped parsley
½ tsp. salt
¼ tsp. pepper
1 egg, beaten
½ cup milk
1 cup bread crumbs, stirred with 2 tbsp. melted butter

Preheat oven to 350 degrees. Layer potatoes, onion, and seasonings in a casserole dish. Combine egg and milk. Pour over potatoes. Cover with bread crumbs. Bake for 30 minutes. Serves 4.

GOLDEN FLECK CASSEROLE

Carrots combine with potatoes to make a colorful and easy casserole. Serve with cold meats for luncheon meals or with any roasts, steaks, or chops for a full-course dinner.

4 medium potatoes, peeled and sliced
4 medium carrots, peeled and sliced
1 medium onion, sliced thinly
2 tbsp. butter
1 can (10-oz.) cream of mushroom soup
1 soup can water

In a greased casserole, layer potatoes, carrots, and onions. Dot with butter. Pour soup and water over the layers. Cover. Bake at 350 degrees for 35 minutes. Uncover and bake 20 minutes longer or until vegetables are tender. Serves 4.

CHEESE-CREAMED POTATOES

This recipe, from the kitchen of Peggy Drummond, Freetown, P.E.I., is a great way to use up leftover cold potatoes. Serve with baked ham and a green vegetable.

3 cups sliced cold potato
2 tbsp. butter
2 tbsp. all-purpose flour
1½ cups milk
1 cup grated cheese
½ tsp. salt
⅛ tsp. pepper

Preheat oven to 400 degrees. Place potatoes in a greased casserole dish. Melt butter in a saucepan. Stir in flour and gradually add milk, grated cheese, and seasonings. Stir over medium heat until thoroughly blended and thickened. Pour over potatoes. Bake until bubbly and browned on top, about 30 minutes. Serves 4.

DRUNKEN POTATOES

Make these in advance and put in the oven at the last minute.

6 medium baking potatoes, peeled and sliced thinly
½ cup vermouth
¼ cup butter or margarine
Salt and pepper to taste

Preheat oven to 375 degrees. Arrange potatoes in greased pie plate, overlapping the slices. Pour vermouth over potatoes and sprinkle with seasonings. Dot with butter. Bake uncovered until tender, 30 to 40 minutes. Serves 6.

POTATOES ALMONDINE

This is a company recipe that is excellent with roast meats. This casserole can be made a day ahead, refrigerated, and reheated.

4 medium potatoes, cooked and mashed
1½ cups cottage cheese
¼ cup sour cream
2 tbsp. chopped green onion
1½ tsp. salt
¼ tsp. pepper
2 tbsp. melted butter
¼ cup slivered almonds

Preheat oven to 350 degrees. Combine mashed potatoes, cottage cheese, sour cream, onion, salt, and pepper. Beat with electric mixer until smooth. Put in a shallow buttered casserole dish. Sprinkle with almonds and brush with melted butter. Bake for 30 minutes. Serves 6 to 8.

SECOND-DAY POTATOES (MICROWAVE)

This is an excellent use for leftover potatoes.

4 medium cooked potatoes, unpeeled
¼ tsp. salt
1 tbsp. dried parsley
½ tsp. marjoram
¼ cup finely chopped onion
1½ cup grated cheddar cheese
¼ cup melted butter

Slice unpeeled potatoes. Arrange in a 1-quart casserole. In a bowl, blend salt, parsley, marjoram, onion, and cheese. Drizzle butter evenly over potatoes. Sprinkle with cheese mixture. Microwave on high for 3 to 5 minutes, rotating halfway through cooking time. Makes 4 to 6 servings.

POTATO PUFF (MICROWAVE)

This airy creation is tasty and easy to prepare.

2 cups hot, mashed potato*
2 eggs, separated
1 cup milk
2 tbsp. softened butter
2 tsp. grated onion
1 tbsp. dried parsley flakes
½ tsp. salt
Dash of pepper
½ cup grated cheddar cheese
Paprika

Beat egg whites until stiff. Blend egg yolks, milk, butter, onion, and seasonings; add to mashed potatoes and mix until well-blended. Fold in beaten egg whites and grated cheese. Gently spoon into buttered 2-quart casserole. Sprinkle with paprika. Place casserole on inverted plate in microwave. Microwave on high 10 to 12 minutes, rotating dish every 5 minutes. For added convenience, use leftover mashed potatoes, reheated in the microwave 2 minutes on high. Serves 4.

Note: Sea captains and sailors ate potatoes for prevention of scurvy. One medium potato contains about 35 percent of an adult's daily requirement of Vitamin C.

POTATO-CHEESE BAKE

This delicious recipe comes from the kitchen of Erma Hickey, of Sherwood Farm Tourist Home at Darnley, P.E.I. Erma tells me she serves this often to her guests along with baked ham and hot curried fruit.

7 to 8 medium potatoes, cooked, peeled, and cubed OR
1 pkg. frozen hash browns
1 can (10½-oz.) cream of chicken soup
1 cup chopped onion
2 cups sour cream
2 cups grated cheddar cheese

Preheat oven to 350 degrees. Combine all ingredients. Place in a large greased casserole dish. Bake until browned on top and heated through. Serves 8.

HOT CURRIED FRUIT*

2 cups fresh or canned peaches
2 cups fresh or canned pears
2 cups fresh or canned apricots
2 cups fresh or canned pineapple
2 tbsp. butter
¼ cup brown sugar
1½ tsp. curry powder
1 can (16-oz.) dark bing cherries

Combine fruits (if using canned fruit, drain well). Stir in butter, brown sugar, and curry powder. Heat in 350-degree oven. (This can be made at the last minute and popped into a microwave for 3 to 4 minutes.) Just before serving, stir in drained cherries.

*Fruits may be substituted to suit individual taste.

COLCANNON

This is a traditional Irish dish. No potato cookbook would be complete without a recipe for this creamy specialty.

3 to 4 medium potatoes, peeled and cut in quarters
2 tbsp. milk or light cream
¼ tsp. salt
⅛ tsp. pepper
2 cups chopped cabbage
2 tbsp. butter or margarine
¼ cup chopped onion
2 tbsp. butter for frying

Cook potatoes in boiling water until tender; drain, reserving water. Place in a large bowl. Beat at medium speed with electric beater until well-mashed. Add milk, salt, and pepper and beat until fluffy. In the same saucepan as potatoes were cooked in, cook cabbage in reserved potato water for 6 to 8 minutes until tender. Drain. Meanwhile, melt 2 tbsp. butter in a frying pan and sautè onion until tender. Add mashed potato and cooked cabbage to the onion. Heat thoroughly, stirring constantly. Place in a heated serving dish. Serve hot, topped with butter. Serves 6.

PRINCESS POTATOES

My friend's German grandmother adapted this recipe to suit Canadian palates. The German dish is called *Prinzesskartoffeln*.

6 medium potatoes, cooked and peeled
2 slices Canadian-style bacon, diced
2 tbsp. chopped onion
2 tbsp. butter
1 tbsp. all-purpose flour
1½ cup milk
Salt and pepper to taste

Cook bacon and onion in butter. Stir in flour and slowly add milk. Cook over low heat until sauce is thickened and smooth. Cut cooked potatoes into half-inch squares; add to sauce. Season to taste with salt and pepper. Serves 6.

POTATO KUGEL

This is a Jewish dish, often served at the Jewish New Year. The potatoes and carrots should be grated by hand or in a food processor. A blender will not give good results. Kugel is best served warm.

5 large potatoes, finely grated
3 medium carrots, finely grated
1 large onion, cut finely
⅓ cup matzoh meal
1 tsp. baking powder
3 eggs, separated
¼ tsp. Tabasco sauce
¼ cup vegetable oil

Combine vegetables; drain off any liquid. Combine matzoh meal and baking powder and stir into vegetables. Beat egg yolks and Tabasco sauce until light; stir into vegetable mixture. Heat oil and quickly stir into other mixture. Fold in stiffly beaten egg whites. Spoon into a greased shallow 9x9" baking dish. Bake at 375 degrees for 1¼ hours, until golden. Let rest 10 minutes before serving. Serves 6.

Note: Frozen French fries are the top-selling frozen food item in most supermarkets in North America.

CHEESY POTATO CAKES

2 cups mashed potato
2 tbsp. minced onion
⅛ tsp. pepper
¼ tsp. salt
2 tbsp. chopped parsley
1 egg, well-beaten
½ cup grated cheddar cheese
¼ cup all-purpose flour or cornmeal

Combine all ingredients. Shape into cakes. Roll in flour or cornmeal. Fry in small amounts of hot fat until golden brown. Makes 6 patties.

LEFSE

Lefse is served buttered and topped with jam or honey. It's a national Norwegian dish that makes a delicious breakfast treat.

2 cups mashed potato (use baking potatoes as they are drier)
2 tbsp. butter
¼ cup cream
½ tsp. granulated sugar
1 tsp. salt
1 cup all-purpose flour
Oil for frying

Combine potato, butter, cream, sugar, and salt. Beat until smooth. Cover and refrigerate until cold. Gradually add flour, working in well by kneading with your hands. Divide the dough into small balls and roll very thinly. Fry in oil in a hot skillet or electric frying pan until browned; turn and brown other side. Put lefse on a large plate and cover with a damp towel while remaining cakes are being cooked. To serve, butter each flat cake, roll loosely and slice in diagonal slices. Sprinkle with extra sugar and top with jam or honey. Yields about 15 (6") cakes.

CRUSTY POTATO LOGS

This is from the kitchen of Brenda Rogers, Linkletter Road, P.E.I.

6 medium potatoes, mashed
¼ cup soft butter
1 tsp. salt
¼ tsp. thyme
⅓ tsp. pepper
3 egg yolks
1 egg, beaten
1 ½ cups crushed corn flakes

Preheat oven to 425 degrees. Combine potato, butter, salt, thyme, pepper, and egg yolks. Beat with an electric mixer until creamy. Shape into logs (about 2 tbsp. of mixture for each). Dip in beaten egg and roll in crushed corn flakes. Place on a greased baking sheet. Bake 15 to 20 minutes. Serve hot. These can be made early in the day, refrigerated, and heated when ready to serve. Makes 12 logs; serves 6.

COMPANY CROQUETTES

This is a nice way to serve potatoes for a company dinner; they're deep-fried and crispy.

2 eggs
2 cups warm mashed potato
½ tsp. salt
Few grains pepper
2 tbsp. butter
¼ tsp. celery salt
1 tbsp. water
¼ cup all-purpose flour
1 cup bread crumbs
Fat for deep frying (375 degrees)

Beat 1 egg. Combine beaten egg, potato, and seasonings. Heat in a saucepan, stirring constantly until mixture leaves the sides of the pan. Cool. Mold into small balls. Beat other egg with water. Roll croquettes in flour, dip in egg, and roll in bread crumbs. Deep fry until well-browned. Serve hot. Makes 12 croquettes.

BARBECUE-HERBED POTATO WEDGES

This recipe from the kitchen of Brenda Rogers makes the nicest herbed potatoes I have eaten. They're excellent with barbecued meats or poultry.

2 tbsp. margarine
¼ cup olive oil
¼ cup chopped onion
3 tbsp. fresh chopped parsley
1 tsp. chili powder
¼ tsp. garlic powder
¼ tsp. basil
¼ tsp. salt
Dash of pepper
6 medium potatoes

Melt margarine and combine with olive oil. Butter a large piece of heavy aluminum foil. Combine chopped onion, herbs, and seasonings. Scrub potatoes and cut in half-inch thick wedges, cutting the potatoes lengthwise. Place potatoes on foil. Brush with margarine and oil mixture. Sprinkle with herbs. Seal the edges of foil. Place on grill about 4" from coals and cook until tender for 30 to 45 minutes. Serves 6.

MAIN-DISH MEALS

All meal-planning centers on the main dish. Potatoes have been chosen by great cooks from around the world to combine with ingredients such as meat, fish, poultry, and cheese in a variety of main-dish meals.

Choose from a collection of fun-to-make, easy-to-serve dishes. The recipes included have many make-ahead meals as well as last-minute, quick-and-easy dishes.

For most of the world, meat and fish are expensive, luxury items. People of North America are fortunate to eat meat or fish nearly every day. However, when any product is readily available, there can be a tendency to waste. Recipes here are geared to prevent waste and save money while providing good nutrition.

Note: in these recipes, peeling potatoes is optional unless specifically stated.

THE POTATO COOKBOOK

MEAT-AND-POTATO LOAF

Serve with cooked vegetables or a green salad.

2 lb. ground beef
2 cups finely shredded potatoes
1 cup crushed soda crackers
1 large onion, chopped
½ cup chopped green pepper
2 eggs
1 cup beef broth (may be made with bouillon cube)
1 tsp. marjoram
½ tsp. basil
¼ tsp. thyme
1 tsp. salt
¼ tsp. pepper

Combine all ingredients. Pour into a 9x5" loaf pan. Bake at 375 degrees for approximately 1 hour. Serves 6 to 8.

OPTIONAL GLAZE

3 tbsp. brown sugar
4 tbsp. ketchup
¼ tsp. nutmeg
1 tsp. dry mustard

Mix together and spread over meat-and-potato mixture before baking.

POTATOBURGER PIE

This hearty meal-in-a-dish comes from England. I like to serve this pie with hot potato biscuits.

1 medium onion, chopped
1 tbsp. vegetable oil
1 lb. ground beef
¾ tsp. salt
Dash of pepper
2 cups drained cooked green beans (or vegetable of your choice)
1 can (10½-oz.) condensed tomato soup
2 cups warm seasoned mashed potato
½ cup grated cheddar cheese (optional)

Preheat oven to 350 degrees. Cook onion in oil until tender but not brown. Add meat and seasonings; brown lightly. Add beans and soup. Pour into a greased 1½-quart casserole dish. Drop mashed potato by spoonfuls on top. If desired, sprinkle with cheese. Bake for 25 to 30 minutes or until browned. Serves 4 to 6.

HOMESTEADERS' BOILED DINNER

Next time you have a baked ham, save the bone while there's still a bit of meat left on it and make an old-fashioned boiled dinner.

1 ham bone (with about 2 cups of meat left on)
2 large onions, quartered
2 cups turnips, cut in wedges
6 carrots, cut in large chunks
6 medium potatoes, quartered
Salt and pepper to taste

Barely cover ham bone with water. Boil until meat falls from the bone. Add onion and turnip, boil 10 minutes; add carrot, boil 10 minutes. Add potatoes and boil until just tender. Season with salt and pepper. (Be careful with salt as there is usually enough in the ham.)

RED FLANNEL HASH

If you happen to have any leftover boiled dinner, drain off the cooking juices and combine any leftover vegetables, mashing with a potato masher. Add any bits of chopped ham. Combine this mixture with an equal quantity of mashed cooked beets. Fry in vegetable oil over medium heat until crusty on the bottom. Turn and heat through. Serve as a quick lunch, with biscuits and chow-chow.

MOCK-DUCK DINNER

This recipe goes back a couple of generations. It was given to me by my sister-in-law, Alberta Reeves of Freetown, P.E.I.

1½ lb. ground beef
2 medium onions, diced
2 cups cubed potato
2 cups sliced carrot
1 cup cubed turnip
2 cups sliced parsnip
4 cups Potato Poultry Dressing (see Miscellaneous)

Brown ground beef loosely in a frying pan. Spread in the bottom of a large baking dish. Simmer vegetables in a small amount of water until barely tender. Drain and spread over ground beef. Top with poultry dressing. Bake at 350 degrees for approximately 30 minutes until thoroughly heated. Serves 4 to 6.

MUSHROOM, PORK, AND POTATO SCALLOP

This casserole may also be cooked in a microwave on medium for 20 minutes, rotating the dish a half-turn after 10 minutes. Let stand 5 minutes before serving if cooked this way.

4 potatoes, peeled and sliced
1 medium onion, sliced
4 pork chops
1 tsp. seasoned salt
¼ tsp. pepper
1 cup sliced fresh mushrooms
1 can (10-oz.) cream of mushroom soup
½ cup milk

Arrange potato and onion slices in a glass baking dish. Place chops on top of vegetables, sprinkle with seasoned salt and pepper, and top with mushrooms. Mix soup and milk; stir until smooth and pour over chops and vegetables. Cover. Bake at 350 degrees for approximately 1 hour. Serves 2 to 4.

PIEROGI CASSEROLE

15 lasagna noodles
2 cups cottage cheese
1 large egg
¼ tsp. onion salt
1 cup shredded cheddar cheese
2 cups mashed potato
¼ tsp. salt
⅛ tsp. pepper
¼ tsp. onion salt
1 cup butter or margarine
1 cup chopped onion

Cook noodles as directed on package. Drain. Spread 5 noodles on the bottom of a 13x9" baking dish. In a medium-sized bowl combine cottage cheese, egg, and onion salt. Spread over noodles. Cover with 5 more noodles. Combine cheddar cheese, potatoes, salt, pepper, and onion salt. Spread over noodles. Cover with remaining noodles. Melt butter in frying pan. Sauté onions slowly until clear and limp. Pour over noodles. Cover. Bake 30 minutes in 350-degree oven. Let stand 10 minutes before cutting. Serve with sour cream. Serves 8.

CORNISH PASTIES

PASTRY

2 cups all-purpose flour
1 cup mashed potato
1 tsp. salt
1 tsp. sugar
¾ cup shortening

MEAT MIXTURE

1 lb. ground beef
2 large potatoes, peeled and diced (¼" cubes)
1 cup finely chopped onion
1 tbsp. freshly chopped parsley
1 tsp. salt
½ tsp. pepper
1 tsp. Worcestershire sauce
¼ tsp. hot pepper sauce

Preheat oven to 375 degrees. Combine flour, potato, salt, sugar, and shortening. Blend with a pastry blender and form into a ball. Divide into 2 equal pieces and roll on a lightly floured board. Cut into 24 5" circles. Combine all other ingredients; mix well. Spoon about 1 tbsp. meat mixture on each circle of pastry; fold and crimp edges to seal the pasties. Bake for 45 minutes or until crust is browned. Serve hot or cold. Can also be reheated. Makes 24 pasties.

PIEROGI

This recipe from Poland yields about 20 pierogi.

CHEESE FILLING

1 cup cottage cheese
1 tsp. melted butter or margarine
3 tbsp. sugar
½ tsp. cinnamon

DOUGH

2 eggs
½ cup water
2 cups all-purpose flour
½ tsp. salt
1 cup cold mashed potato

Water for boiling
Butter or margarine
Breadcrumbs

FILLING: Cream cheese with melted butter. Add sugar and cinnamon and mix well.

DOUGH: Combine all ingredients in a bowl and blend until barely mixed. Divide dough in half and roll thinly on a floured board. Cut into circles with a large cookie cutter. Place a small amount of filling on one side of circle. Moisten the edges of circle with water and fold dough over filling. Press edges firmly together. Seal edges well to keep filling from running out. Press with fork tines. Carefully drop pierogi into boiling salted water, using a slotted spoon. Do not overcrowd. Cook about 12 minutes. Drain. Fry in butter before serving and sprinkle with fine bread crumbs. Serves 4 to 6.

DUCHESS SAUTEED BEEF LIVER

This recipe from France turns liver and onions into a celebration.

2 egg yolks
4 cups mashed potato, seasoned with salt and pepper
¼ cup all-purpose flour
1½ tsp. salt
¼ tsp. pepper
1½ lb. sliced beef liver
2 tbsp. vegetable oil
2 medium onions, sliced
1 green pepper, seeded and cut in wedges
1 tomato, cut in thin slices
1½ cups water
1 tbsp. beef bouillon base

Preheat oven to 400 degrees. Beat egg yolk into mashed potato. Pipe potato in a border around the edge of a large casserole or baking dish. (If you do not have a pastry bag, use an ice-cream scoop to make small mounds around the dish.) Bake for 15 minutes, until heated through. Meanwhile, combine flour, salt, and pepper on waxed paper. Cut liver in serving-sized pieces and coat with flour. Sauté liver in hot oil in a large skillet for 4 minutes on each side. In casserole arrange slices in an overlapping fashion inside the border of potatoes. Turn oven temperature to lowest possible setting and keep liver and potato mixture warm. Sauté onion and green peppers in the same skillet, adding more oil if necessary, for about 10 minutes. Slice tomatoes and add to the skillet. Sauté 2 minutes longer. Arrange vegetables on top of liver. Add water and soup base to skillet. Bring to a boil, stirring and scraping the pan to dissolve any brown bits. Simmer uncovered. Pour over liver. Serve at once. Serves 4 to 6.

Note: Some Bhutanese blamed the potato for stomach problems. It was found later that they were eaten with large helpings of hot chili peppers.

SPICY BEEF AND POTATO HOT POT

Makes 4 generous servings with only 1 pound of steak. Serve with cheese biscuits, hot from the oven.

1 lb. boneless steak, cut in small cubes
2 tbsp. all-purpose flour
2 tbsp. vegetable oil
1 medium onion, chopped
½ cup chopped celery
1 clove garlic, minced
4 to 5 medium potatoes, peeled and cubed
1 can (8-oz.) tomato sauce
½ cup water
2 tbsp. cider vinegar
1 tbsp. Worcestershire sauce
2 tsp. dry mustard
¼ tsp. Tabasco sauce
Dash ground red pepper
Salt and pepper to taste

Preheat oven to 350 degrees. Coat meat with flour. Heat oil in a large skillet over medium heat. Cook meat until browned. Add onion, celery, and garlic. Cook until limp. Add remaining ingredients. Cook until meat and potatoes are well-coated with spices and oil. Place in a 2-quart casserole dish. Cover and bake for 1½ hours until meat and potatoes are tender. Serves 4.

Note: Some potatoes take longer to cook than others. I find Russet Burbanks take nearly 2 hours to cook in this casserole.

Note: In England, potatoes were once thought to "increase seed and provoke lust."

POT ROAST SUPREME

1 3-lb. boneless rump roast
1 tbsp. vegetable oil
2 cups beef bouillon
1 tbsp. horseradish
1 bay leaf
1 clove garlic, minced
3 medium carrots, cut in 2" pieces
6 medium potatoes, peeled and quartered
1 small turnip, peeled and cut in large cubes
1 medium cabbage (about 2 lb.) cut in 6 wedges
½ cup water
1 tbsp. cornstarch

In a large saucepan or Dutch oven, brown meat in oil. Pour off any excess fat and discard. Add bouillon, horseradish, bay leaf, and garlic; cover and cook over low heat. After about 2 hours, add carrot, potatoes, and turnip. Cook 30 minutes, stirring occasionally. Set cabbage on top of other ingredients (without stirring) and cook 30 minutes longer. Remove bay leaf before serving. Remove meat and vegetables and place on a serving platter; keep warm. Meanwhile, blend water with cornstarch until smooth. Slowly stir into cooking liquid. Cook, stirring until thickened. Pour over meat and vegetables on platter. Serve at once. Serves 6 to 8.

Note: Hollywood used flaked potatoes to simulate snow in their early movies.

POTATO PATCHWORK CASSEROLE

This casserole freezes well. I like to double the recipe and freeze half.

1 lb. ground beef
1 medium green pepper, chopped
½ cup chopped onion
4 cups cubed cooked potatoes
1 can (8-oz.) tomato sauce
1 can (3-oz.) tomato paste
½ cup water
½ tsp. salt
Dash pepper
¼ tsp. basil
2 cups thinly sliced cheddar cheese

Preheat oven to 350 degrees. Brown meat loosely in a frying pan. Add green pepper and onion and cook until tender. Stir in potatoes, tomato sauce, tomato paste, water, salt, pepper, and basil. Spoon half of this mixture into a baking dish. Cover with half the cheese slices. Top with remaining potato mixture. Cover dish and bake in preheated oven for 45 minutes. Uncover. Top with remaining cheese slices, cut in decorative shapes, and arrange in a patchwork design. Let stand 5 minutes or until cheese melts. Serve hot. Serves 6.

CHRISTMAS TOURTIERE

This prize-winning recipe makes a delicious Christmas Eve buffet dish, served with cranberry sauce and tossed salad.

Pastry for 2 double-crust pies
1½ lb. minced pork
1 clove garlic, minced
1 medium cooking onion, diced
½ tsp. thyme
½ tsp. sage
¼ tsp. ginger
½ tsp. dry mustard
⅛ tsp. cloves
1½ tsp. salt
½ tsp. allspice
2 medium potatoes, mashed
½ cup potato water

Combine pork, garlic, onion, and seasonings in a frying pan. Cook until meat is tender. Add mashed potato and stir. Cool. Preheat oven to 400 degrees. Line 2 pie plates with pastry. Pour filling into pie plates; cover with remaining pastry. Slash top to allow steam to escape. Bake until crust is brown. These pies freeze well after baking, or can be prepared, frozen (unbaked), and baked when needed. Each pie serves 6.

OLDE ENGLISH MEAT PIE

This is a meat pie with a difference—this tasty recipe uses beef liver.

1 lb. beef liver
¼ cup all-purpose flour
1 tsp. salt
¼ tsp. pepper
¼ cup vegetable oil
2½ cups sliced carrot
4 to 5 medium potatoes, sliced
1½ cups sliced onion
2 tsp. instant beef broth
½ tsp. sage or thyme

Cut beef liver into 1½" squares; coat with a mixture of flour, salt, and pepper. Brown liver a bit at a time in hot oil in a large skillet. Remove with a slotted spoon to an 8-cup casserole dish. Pare and slice carrot and potatoes; cook in salt water (barely to top of vegetables) for 10 minutes. Remove with a slotted spoon to casserole, reserving liquid. Sauté onions in drippings in skillet until soft. Add water to vegetable cooking liquid to make 2 cups; stir into skillet with beef broth and sage or thyme. Pour over vegetables and liver in casserole. Bake at 400 degrees for about 40 minutes. Serves 6.

Note: Almost any part of a potato can produce more potatoes; seed pieces, true potato seed, or cuttings from the plant.

OLD-FASHIONED TURKEY VEGETABLE PIE

This is an excellent way to serve that leftover Christmas turkey.

Pastry or biscuit dough to cover a 2½-quart casserole
3 cups cubed leftover cooked turkey
3 cups cubed cooked potatoes
1 cup diced carrot
½ cup chopped onion
½ cup chopped celery
½ cup finely cubed turnip
½ tsp. salt
¼ tsp. pepper
¼ tsp. oregano
1 cup water
⅔ cup thawed frozen peas
2 cups leftover turkey gravy OR
1 can (10-oz.) cream of celery soup

Preheat oven to 350 degrees. Place turkey, potato, carrot, onion, celery, and turnip in a casserole dish. Sprinkle with seasonings. Add water and stir. Cover and bake at 350 degrees for 1 hour. Add peas and bake another 15 minutes. Drain liquid from casserole and combine with gravy or soup. Pour over casserole. Cover with pie crust or biscuit topping. Slash top to let steam escape. Bake at 425 degrees for 20 minutes or until golden brown. Serves 6.

Note: In Indonesia, potatoes are reserved for special occasions, such as weddings and birthdays.

RAPURE

This is a popular Acadian recipe.

18 large potatoes
1 cup hot mashed potato
2 cups bread crumbs
1½ tsp. salt
Pepper to taste
2 medium onions, chopped finely
½ cup rendered pork fat
4- to 5-lb. stewing chicken, cooked and cut in small pieces
⅓ cup milk
2 eggs
2 tbsp. baking powder

Peel potatoes and grate very finely. Drain liquid. Preheat oven to 350 degrees. Add mashed potato, bread crumbs, salt, and pepper to grated potatoes. Sauté onion in a small amount of pork fat. Combine chicken and onion with potato mixture. Beat milk, eggs, and baking powder and mix with other ingredients. Put remaining pork fat in a large pan (12x16") and heat. Mix about half the fat into potato mixture. Pour mixture into hot pan; pour over remaining fat. Bake for 2 hours or until brown and crusty. Cut in squares and serve with molasses. Serves 10 to 12.

Note: Variation: Cubed cooked pork may be used in place of chicken, or recipe can be made without meat.

HUNGARIAN GOULASH

One cup of light cream may be substituted for the canned tomatoes in this recipe.

2 lb. beef, cut in 1" cubes
2 medium onions, thinly sliced
½ cup margarine or butter
1 tsp. salt
¼ tsp. pepper
½ tsp. paprika
1 cup canned tomatoes
4 medium potatoes, diced

Sauté meat and onions in margarine until browned. Add seasonings and tomatoes. Simmer for 30 minutes. Add potatoes and simmer an additional 30 minutes. Serves 6.

Note: If goulash seems too dry, add ¼ to ½ cup water.

CHICKEN-POTATO STIR FRY

Fries go Oriental when stirred up with chicken and snow peas. This recipe comes from the Potato Board of Denver, Colorado.

6 to 8 oz. skinned and boned chicken breasts
4 tsp. cornstarch
1 clove garlic, halved
2 tbsp. vegetable oil
1½ cups frozen French fries
1½ cups trimmed snow peas
1 cup sliced mushrooms
⅓ cup teriyaki sauce
⅓ cup water
1 medium tomato, cut into wedges

Pound chicken breasts with a rolling pin to flatten slightly. Cut into ¼" strips. Toss with cornstarch to coat; set aside. In a large wok or skillet, over high heat cook garlic in 1 tbsp. oil until lightly browned. Discard garlic. Add frozen French fries to wok; stir fry about 5 minutes until lightly browned and cooked through. Remove with a slotted spoon to paper towels. Heat the remaining oil in wok. Add chicken. Stir fry over high heat for 2 minutes. Add snow peas and mushrooms. Stir fry about 3 minutes, until chicken is opaque and snow peas are tender-crisp. Stir in teriyaki sauce and water. Add tomato and reserved potatoes. Toss gently, just until heated through. Serve immediately. Serves 2.

CHICKEN FRICOT (WITH DUMPLINGS)

An ever-popular Acadian dish dating back to the early pioneers, this recipe comes from Rita Arsenault of Abram's Village, P.E.I.

1 broiler chicken, cut in serving-sized pieces
¼ cup butter or margarine
1 medium onion, chopped
6 cups water
4 to 5 cups peeled and cubed potatoes
1 tbsp. salt
Pepper to taste

In a large saucepan, fry chicken slowly in butter for about 30 minutes. Add chopped onion and fry another 10 to 15 minutes. Cover with boiling water. Cover pot and simmer until chicken is lightly tender. Add potatoes, salt, and pepper and continue cooking while preparing dumplings.

DUMPLINGS

1 cup all-purpose flour
¼ tsp. salt
1½ tsp. baking powder
Cold water

Combine flour, salt, baking powder, and enough water to make a soft, slightly sticky dough. Drop dumplings by teaspoon into fricot. Cover and cook an additional 15 minutes. Do not remove cover while dumplings are cooking. Serve hot. Serves 6 to 8.

MEREDITH'S MASHIE BURGERS

"Leftover mashed potatoes are prized in the Potato Museum kitchen," according to Meredith Hughes. "They form a thickener for soups, add moisture and minerals to muffins, and mixed with chopped vegetables and fried will feed the hungry hordes as Meredith's Mashie Burgers."

2 cups leftover mashed potato
1 egg, lightly beaten
2 tbsp. whole wheat flour
½ cup chopped scallions
2 tbsp. fresh chopped parsley
¾ cup grated cheddar cheese
½ cup chopped walnuts
½ cup chopped mushrooms
1 large carrot, grated
Freshly ground black pepper
Salt to taste
Heaping tbsp. chopped fresh dill (optional)
Olive oil for frying

Combine all ingredients in a large bowl, mixing them as you would a meat-loaf preparation. Form into patties and fry on both sides in olive oil until lightly browned. Serve on hamburger rolls or toasted bread. Makes 6 burgers.

ALL-PURPOSE HASH

Almost any meat or fish will make a delicious hash. It's a super way to use left-over roast beef, poultry, pork, ham, corned beef, or fish.

1 cup chopped onion
1 clove garlic, crushed (optional)
¼ cup butter or margarine
2 tbsp. bacon drippings or vegetable oil
4 medium potatoes, cooked and cubed
½ tsp. salt
¼ tsp. pepper
¼ tsp. thyme
3 cups cubed cooked meat
2 tbsp. water

Sauté onion and garlic in butter and bacon drippings until tender. Add potatoes, salt, pepper, and thyme. Cook over medium heat until potatoes are golden. Add meat and water. Heat thoroughly. Serves 6.

Note: Variation: Form hash into small mounds (about the size of a hamburger patty). Hollow slightly in center. Add an egg to each mound. Cover and simmer 3 to 4 minutes, until eggs are set.

HOUSE BANKIN'

This easily prepared pioneer recipe is sure to please.

1 lb. salt cod
4 medium raw potatoes, sliced
6 slices bacon
1 large onion, sliced

Soak cod for 3 hours in cold water. Cut into small pieces. Drain, cover with cold water and simmer over low heat for 15 minutes. Add peeled, sliced potatoes and cook until potatoes are tender. Meanwhile, cut bacon into small pieces and fry until crisp. Remove from pan and set aside. Sauté onion rings in pan drippings until soft and clear. Drain fish and potatoes. Place in a serving bowl. Pour bacon, onion, and drippings over the fish. Serve immediately while very hot with bannock and molasses. Serves 4 to 6.

WHITE FISH SOUFFLE

Almost any white fish can be used for this dish. It's easy and economical.

1 lb. cold cooked fish, flaked
2 tbsp. grated carrot
2 tbsp. grated onion
½ tsp. salt
½ tsp. pepper
4 eggs, separated
2 cups mashed potato (seasoned to taste with salt and pepper)
2 tbsp. melted butter or margarine

Preheat oven to 350 degrees. Combine fish, carrot, onion, salt, and pepper. Beat egg yolks and add to this mixture. Stir in mashed potato and melted butter. Fold in stiffly beaten egg whites. Spread in a greased baking dish. Set in a pan of warm water in the center of the oven. Bake 30 minutes.
Serves 4 to 6.

QUICK FISH CAKES

Canned chicken haddie makes these fish cakes quick to make.

2 medium onions, chopped
¹/₃ cup water
2 cups chicken haddie, drained and flaked
8 medium potatoes, cooked and mashed
4 parsnips, cooked and mashed
¹/₂ tsp. salt (or to taste)
¹/₄ tsp. pepper
1 egg, well beaten
¹/₂ cup fine bread crumbs
Fat for frying (such as bacon drippings)

Cook onions in water. Do not drain. Add fish and vegetables; season with salt and pepper. Add egg and mix well. Form into patties. Roll in bread crumbs. Fry in bacon drippings or other fat. Makes 12 to 16 patties.

SEA CAKES

This is a recipe from the P.E.I. Department of Fisheries.

1 can (15-oz.) mackerel
¹/₄ cup chopped onion
1 egg, beaten
2 cups mashed potato
1 tsp. salt
¹/₂ tsp. pepper
1 tbsp. ketchup
1 cup dry bread crumbs
¹/₂ cup melted butter or margarine

Preheat oven to 450 degrees. Rinse, drain, skin, and flake mackerel. Combine fish, onion, egg, potatoes, salt, pepper, and ketchup. Mix well. Shape into 12 cakes and roll in bread crumbs. Place on a well-greased baking pan. Brush with melted margarine. Bake for 8 minutes, or until browned on bottom. Turn carefully and bake 3 to 5 minutes longer or until brown on both sides. Serves 6.

BUFFET SEAFOOD ELEGANTE

⅓ cup butter or margarine
1 small onion, chopped
2 tbsp. all-purpose flour
1 ⅛ cups milk
3 raw potatoes, peeled and sliced
½ lb. white fish fillets, cut in pieces
1 small can (7-oz.) shrimp, drained
1 tsp. dry parsley
1 can (10-oz.) sliced mushrooms, drained

Cook onion in melted butter over medium heat until transparent. Gradually stir in flour, blending well. Cook 1 minute, stirring constantly. Slowly add milk and cook until mixture is smooth and thick, stirring constantly. Line a buttered casserole with potato slices. Arrange fish and shrimp over potatoes. Sprinkle with parsley and mushrooms. Pour sauce over the casserole and place in oven. Cook 40 minutes at 375 degrees until potatoes are tender. Serves 4 to 6.

Note: Before the convenience of electric heating and cooking stoves, Grandma used to throw raw potato peelings in her wood stove and fireplace to remove soot and creosote build-up. I don't know why this works, but I've tried it and it does.

TUNA PUFF CASSEROLE

This light and delicious casserole combines 2 old favorites, potatoes and tuna.

2 cans (7-oz.) tuna, drained and flaked
2 tbsp. finely minced onion
2 tbsp. chopped fresh parsley
Dash pepper
1 cup cooked peas
4 cups mashed potato
2 egg yolks
2 egg whites
2 tbsp. melted butter or margarine
½ tsp. salt

Combine tuna, onion, parsley, pepper, peas, potatoes, and egg yolks. Mix well. Beat egg whites until soft peaks form; add to potato and fish mixture. Mix in melted butter and salt. Put in a greased casserole and bake at 450 degrees for 20 minutes until nicely browned. Serves 4.

Note: Variation: Salmon may be used instead of tuna.

SCOTTISH SHEPHERD'S PIE

A traditional dish from Scotland, this pie is easy to prepare and always welcome.

½ lb. chopped cooked beef
1 small onion, cooked and chopped
1 tsp. ketchup
Salt and pepper to taste
1 cup leftover gravy
2 cups seasoned mashed potato
2 tbsp. butter or margarine
Cayenne pepper
Parsley flakes

Preheat oven to 350 degrees. Mix together meat, onion, ketchup, salt, pepper, and gravy. Place in a greased baking dish. Cover with mashed potato. Dot with small pieces of butter. Bake for 20 to 30 minutes. Sprinkle with cayenne pepper and decorate with a little parsley. Serve hot. Serves 2.

Note: Variation: This pie can be made using any type of meat and gravy, or by substituting cooked white fish and a tasty white sauce or creamed soup for the meat and gravy.

CLAM CASSEROLE

½ cup melted butter or margarine
2 tbsp. all-purpose flour
1 cup evaporated milk
2 small cans (10-oz.) baby clams and juice
1 cup finely chopped onion
3 cups diced raw potato
1 tsp. salt
¼ tsp. pepper
1 tsp. celery seed
2 tbsp. parsley flakes
4 hard-cooked eggs, quartered
1 cup soft bread crumbs

Melt butter and put in the bottom of a casserole dish. Add flour and mix until blended. Stir in milk and clam juice; mix well to dissolve any lumps. Add clams, onion, potato, and seasonings. Mix into sauce. Gently mix in hard-cooked eggs so as to not break them up. Sprinkle with breadcrumbs. Bake covered for 20 minutes at 350 degrees. Remove cover and bake until potato is cooked and casserole is lightly browned on top. Serves 6.

FISH AND POTATO SCALLOP

P.E.I.'s most popular foods combine for a new twist to an old favorite.

1 lb. white fish (cod, haddock, sole, for example)
2 tbsp. lemon juice
¼ cup butter or margarine, divided
2 tbsp. all-purpose flour
2 cups milk
1½ tsp. finely minced onion
1 tsp. salt
¼ tsp. pepper
2 cups peas and carrots (partially cooked)
4 cups diced potato (partially cooked)
⅛ tsp. nutmeg
¾ cup cracker crumbs

Partially cook potatoes in a small amount of water. Drain. Cut fish into 1" cubes. Cover with boiling water and lemon juice. Heat 2 tbsp. margarine. Add flour and stir until bubbling. Stir in onion and milk. Cook until thick in a double boiler. Season with salt and pepper. Fold in partially cooked vegetables and nutmeg. Drain fish. Mix fish with the vegetable mixture. Place in a casserole. Bake at 350 degrees for 30 to 45 minutes or until vegetables are cooked through. Serves 6.

Note: Potatoes are hailed as a cure for gout, lumbago, black eyes, sunburn, rheumatism, sore throats, toothaches, temper tantrums, and drunkenness.

Potatoes have been said to cause rickets, indigestion, syphilis, leprosy, lust, and warts.

MISCELLANEOUS

This section will show the diverse qualities of the potato. Here, in a collection of recipes that includes pancake syrup, mayonnaise, hot chocolate, pizza, pastry, and pudding sauce to name a few, we find the ever-capable potato.

Note: Save bread as it begins to dry out. I use bread that is about 3 days old. Chop in a blender and store in a glass jar. Bread crumbs that are dried properly will keep several weeks.

THE POTATO COOKBOOK

POTATO WATER

Because I usually save potato water in a container in my refrigerator, I don't generally have to "make" potato water. But just in case, here is the way to get the most nutrients from your potatoes.

2 medium potatoes
2½ cups water

Boil potatoes with peelings on. Be careful not to cook too long; if potatoes break up, water will be cloudy. Do not cut potatoes before cooking. Water should look much like apple juice.

POTATO PASTRY

1½ cups all-purpose flour
½ tsp. salt
½ cup lard or shortening
¼ cup mashed potato
1 egg yolk

Preheat oven to 350 degrees. Combine flour and salt and cut in lard until mixture is crumbly. Add mashed potato and egg yolk. Toss with a fork until a ball is formed. (Do not add water.) Divide into 2 balls. Roll with a light even pressure to form a circle an inch larger than the inverted pie plate. Place pastry in pie plate. Prick with a fork and bake 12 to 15 minutes. Makes 2 9" pie shells or 1 double-crust pie.

NEVER-FAIL POTATO PASTRY

This light and buttery "Never-Fail" pastry is from Australia.

2½ cups all-purpose flour
½ tsp. salt
1 tsp. baking powder
1 cup butter or margarine
⅔ cup mashed potato

Sift together flour, salt, and baking powder. Add butter and blend with a pastry blender until mixture resembles fine crumbs. Add potato and blend with the pastry blender or fork until well-mixed. Place in refrigerator for at least 1 hour before using. Preheat oven to 450 degrees. Roll on a floured board. Fit into a pie plate and prick with a fork. Bake for 10 minutes. Fill with desired filling. Makes 2 9" pie shells.

POTATO POULTRY DRESSING

This recipe makes enough dressing for 1 large chicken or small turkey.

⅓ cup butter or margarine
1½ cups chopped onion
1½ cups chopped celery
1½ tsp. salt
⅛ tsp. pepper
½ tsp. poultry seasoning
½ tsp. sage
6 cups bread cubes
¼ cup water
1 egg, beaten
2 cups mashed potato

Melt butter; sauté onion and celery. Combine with remaining ingredients. Toss lightly. Use to stuff a large chicken or small turkey. Serves 6.

POTATO MAPLE SYRUP

Try this delicious, economical syrup on ice cream, pancakes, or in recipes such as Potato Syrup Pie. Keeps well in refrigerator.

2 cups clear potato water
2 cups granulated sugar
Few shakes salt
1 tsp. maple flavoring

Combine potato water, sugar and salt. Bring to a full rolling boil and boil rapidly for 10 minutes. Add maple flavoring. Cool. Store in a glass bottle in refrigerator for up to 4 months. Makes 2 cups.

POTATO MAYONNAISE

Serve with cold meat. Keep refrigerated.

1 cup mashed potato
4 tbsp. olive oil or salad oil
6 tbsp. vinegar
2 tsp. horseradish
1 tsp. Worcestershire sauce
½ tsp. salt
½ tsp. dry mustard
½ tsp. granulated sugar

Combine all ingredients and mix well. Keeps for up to 2 weeks in refrigerator. Makes 1½ cups.

CHOCOLATE SYRUP

Great on ice cream or to add to hot or cold milk, this syrup will keep for weeks in the refrigerator.

½ cup cocoa
1½ cups granulated sugar
1½ cups boiling potato water
1½ tsp. cornstarch
Small amount of cold water
1½ tsp. vanilla

Mix cocoa and sugar; sift if lumpy. Add boiling potato water. Boil rapidly for 3 minutes. Mix cornstarch with cold water. Add to chocolate mixture. Simmer 5 minutes. Add vanilla. Cool. Makes 2 cups.

POTATO-WATER PUDDING SAUCE

There is no end to the ways you can use this easy pudding sauce recipe. Try it on Cottage Pudding, Carrot and Potato Pudding, or Blueberry Cake, to name a few.

1 cup brown sugar
⅛ tsp. salt
2 tbsp. cornstarch
2 cups potato water
1½ tsp. vanilla
1 tsp. lemon juice
1 tbsp. butter or margarine

Mix brown sugar, salt, and cornstarch. Add potato water. Bring to a boil. Simmer until thick and clear. Add vanilla, lemon juice, and butter; stir. Serve hot. Makes 2 cups.

POTATO PIZZA

This recipe comes from Australia. It's a quick-to-make pizza that is chock full of flavor.

CRUST

1 cup cooked sieved potato
2 tbsp. melted butter or margarine
2 tbsp. milk
½ tsp. salt
1 cup all-purpose flour
½ tsp. baking powder

TOPPING

1 medium onion, finely chopped
½ cup sliced mushrooms
2 tbsp. butter or margarine
1 large tomato, thinly sliced
1 cup grated parmesan cheese

Prepare crust by beating together potato, butter, milk, and salt. Add flour and baking powder to make a stiff dough. Sauté onion and mushrooms in butter. Cut dough into 5 4" circles and cook on a griddle or greased skillet until browned lightly. Transfer to a baking sheet. Place grated cheese and sliced tomatoes on crust. Cover with sautéed onions and mushrooms and sprinkle with parmesan cheese. Brown under a hot broiler. Makes 5 mini-pizzas.

Note: In a good year, the Russians are credited with approximately ⅓ of the world's potato production. Potatoes are called "the second bread of Russia."

TURKEY STUFFING

A delicious full-flavored stuffing, this can be baked in a casserole or used to stuff a 12- to 15-pound turkey.

1 large onion, minced
½ cup butter or margarine
6 cups mashed potato
6 cups dry bread crumbs
¼ cup chicken soup base powder
½ tsp. pepper
1 tbsp. poultry seasoning
(This recipe requires no extra salt other than that contained in the soup base.)

Preheat oven to 350 degrees. Sauté onion in butter over low heat until barely tender. Do not brown. Mix well with remaining ingredients. Place in a greased casserole and bake for 30 minutes or use to stuff the cavity in a turkey and cook in the usual manner.

MOCK ALMOND PASTE

This recipe was given to me by a professional cake decorator from Vancouver, British Columbia. She uses it regularly in her shop. It's lovely for wedding and Christmas cakes.

½ cup mashed potato
½ cup margarine or butter
2 lb. icing sugar
Almond flavoring to taste (about 1 tsp.)

Beat potato in a mixer until smooth. Add margarine and gradually mix in flavoring and sugar. When too stiff to beat, put on a counter and knead in the rest of the sugar.

POTATO CHIP CRUNCH SANDWICH

This recipe comes from the kitchen of Cindy Chase of Halifax, Nova Scotia. It's a healthy snack for young and old alike.

>   **4 strips bacon, cut in half**
>   **8 slices cracked or whole wheat bread**
>   **Soft butter or margarine**
>   **Peanut butter**
>   **1 small bag of potato chips**

Sauté bacon until nicely browned. Drain on absorbent paper. Butter 4 slices of bread. Spread peanut butter on remaining bread. Arrange a triple layer of potato chips over peanut butter (good way to use up broken chips). Put 2 pieces of bacon on each sandwich. Cover with buttered bread. Garnish with pickle or radish roses. Serves 2.

POTATO NOODLES

Next time you serve Stroganoff, try these delicious buttery noodles. This recipe was adapted from a popular Hungarian dish.

>   **5 medium potatoes**
>   **1½ tsp. salt**
>   **2 eggs**
>   **1 cup all-purpose flour**
>   **4 to 6 tbsp. butter or margarine**

Boil whole unpeeled potatoes in a small amount of water. Drain. Peel and rice or mash. Add salt, eggs, and flour to hot potatoes. Knead on a lightly floured board until dough is easy to roll. Add extra flour if necessary. Preheat oven to 375 degrees. Roll dough as thinly as possible. Cut into strips about ¼x4". Let dry for about 20 minutes. Layer noodles in a criss-crossed fashion in a buttered baking dish. Dot with remaining butter. Bake uncovered until nicely browned, 25 to 30 minutes. Serves 5 to 6.

POTATO SUBMARINES

This is a good choice for hearty teenage appetites, and it's highly nutritious.

2 cups cooked and diced potatoes
½ cup mayonnaise
1 tsp. prepared mustard
¼ cup chopped onion
⅓ cup shredded cheese
¾ cup chopped celery
1 can sardines, drained and chopped
2 hard-cooked eggs, chopped
1 tsp. salt
¼ tsp. pepper
3 small-sized submarine buns
1 dill pickle, seeded and sliced into 6
    equal pieces for garnish

Add mayonnaise and mustard to potatoes and let stand 15 minutes. Combine onion, cheese, celery, sardines, eggs, salt, and pepper. Mix potatoes with other ingredients. Halve submarine rolls down the center lengthwise. Spoon in the potato mixture. Garnish with dill pickle. Serves 6.

APPENDIX

Ingredient Substitutions

1 tsp. *baking powder* (double acting) = 1½ tsp. regular baking powder

1 tsp. *baking powder* = ¼ tsp. baking soda plus ½ tsp. cream of tartar

1 cup *butter* = 1 cup margarine
        or ⅞ cup shortening plus ¼ tsp. salt
        or ⅞ cup lard plus ¼ tsp. salt

1 oz. unsweetened *chocolate* = 3 level tbsp. cocoa plus 1 tbsp. butter, margarine,
        or shortening

1 tbsp. *cornstarch* (for thickening) = 2 tbsp. flour or 4 tbsp. tapioca

1 cup *corn syrup* = 1 cup honey or molasses or 1 cup sugar plus ¼ cup liquid
        (*Note.* Do not substitute corn syrup when making candies)

¾ cup *cracker crumbs* = 1 cup bread crumbs

Cream: 1 cup *coffee cream* = ⅞ cup milk plus 3 tbsp. butter
            1 cup *heavy cream* = ¾ cup milk plus ⅓ cup butter
            1 cup *sour cream* (heavy) = ⅔ cup sour milk plus ⅓ cup butter
            1 cup *sour cream* (light) = ¾ cup sour milk plus 3 tbsp. butter
            1 cup *sweet cream* = ¾ cup milk plus ¼ cup butter

Eggs: Never substitute anything for eggs; however . . .
            1 whole egg = 2 egg yolks (for thickening)
            1 whole egg = 2 egg yolks plus 2 tbsp. water (in cookies)
            2 large eggs = 3 small eggs
            1 cup whole eggs = 5 to 6 large eggs
            1 cup egg whites = whites of 8 to 10 large eggs
            1 cup egg yolks = yolks of 12 large eggs

Flour: 1 cup sifted *all-purpose flour* = 1 cup plus 2 tbsp. cake or pastry flour
            1 cup *pastry flour* = 1 cup minus 2 tbsp. all-purpose flour
            1 cup *flour (for breads)* = ½ cup bran, whole wheat flour, or cornmeal
               plus ½ cup all-purpose flour
            1 cup *unsifted flour* = 1 cup plus 2 tbsp. sifted flour
            1 cup *self-rising* flour = 1 cup sifted all-purpose flour plus 1½ tsp. bak-
               ing powder and ¼ tsp. salt

1 clove *garlic* = ⅛ tsp. garlic powder

1 tbsp. *fresh herbs* (parsley flakes, oregano, etc.) = 1 tsp. dried herbs

1 cup liquid *honey* = 1 cup corn syrup
        or 1 cup molasses

or 1 cup sugar plus ¼ cup liquid (i.e., water, milk—whatever liquid recipe calls for)

1 cup *ketchup* = 1 cup tomato sauce plus ½ cup sugar and 2 tbsp. vinegar

Juice of 1 *lemon* = 3 to 4 tbsp. bottled lemon juice

1 cup *meat stock* = 1 bouillon cube plus 1 cup water

or 1 cup consommé

or 1 rounded tsp. soup base powder in 1 cup water

Milk: 1 cup *skim milk* = 1 cup water plus 4 tbsp. powdered milk

1 cup *sour milk* = 1 cup buttermilk

or

1 tbsp. vinegar or lemon juice and enough milk to fill 1 cup (let stand several minutes)

1 cup *sweet milk* = ½ cup evaporated milk plus ½ cup water

or

(for baking) 1 cup sour milk plus ½ tsp. baking soda (decrease baking powder in recipe by 2 tsp.)

or

1 cup reconstituted dry milk plus 2 tbsp. margarine

**Never substitute anything for sweetened condensed milk

1 tsp. dry *mustard* = 1 tbsp. prepared mustard

**Never substitute oil for shortening or vice versa (except in frying)

1 small fresh *onion* = 1 tbsp. onion flakes or minced instant onion

Juice of 1 *orange* = ⅓ cup reconstituted orange juice

Sugar: 1 cup *granulated sugar* = 1 cup brown sugar, firmly packed

1 cup *sugar* = ¾ cup honey

or

1 cup molasses plus ¼ tsp. soda (reduce liquid in recipe by ¼ cup)

4 tbsp. *tapioca* (to thicken) = 2 tbsp. flour or 1 tbsp. cornstarch

1 cup canned *tomatoes* = 1⅓ cups fresh tomatoes, peeled and simmered for 10 minutes

1 cup *tomato juice* = ½ cup tomato sauce plus ½ cup water

1 cup *tomato sauce* = ½ cup tomato paste plus ½ cup water

1 tbsp. *yeast* = 1 envelope dry yeast or 1 cake yeast

1 cup *yogurt* = 1 cup sour milk

Temperature Chart for Deep-Frying

	Temperature of fat (in degrees)	Time in minutes
Croquettes (previously cooked food)	375	2 to 4
Doughnuts	375	2 to 3
Fritters	365-375	3 to 5
French fries	370	7
Vegetable rings	375-380	3
Oysters or small fish	375	2 to 5

Oven Temperature Chart

	Fahrenheit	Celsius
Very slow oven	250-300	120-150
Slow oven	300-325	150-160
Moderate oven	325-375	160-190
Moderately hot oven	375-400	190-200
Hot oven	400-450	200-230
Very hot oven	450-500	230-260

Approximate Baking Times in a Preheated Oven

Note: This is an approximate guide. Follow baking times and temperatures given in individual recipes.

	Temperature (degrees)	Time
Breads:		
coffee cakes	375	20 to 25 minutes
cornbread	375	30 minutes
fruit & nut loaves	350	1 hour
muffins	375	30 minutes
popovers	450	15 minutes, then

THE POTATO COOKBOOK

	350	20 minutes
tea biscuits	425	12 to 15 minutes
yeast loaves	375	30 minutes
yeast rolls	350	15 to 20 minutes

Cakes:

angel food	375	30 minutes
butter (layer)	350	25 to 30 minutes
butter (square)	350	50 to 60 minutes
cake mix	350	30 to 35 minutes
chiffon	325	1 hour
cup cakes	350	20 to 25 minutes
fruit cakes	275	1½ to 3 hours, depending on size of cake
gingerbread	325	50 to 60 minutes
jelly roll	325	15 minutes
pound cake	325	1 to 1¼ hours
sponge cake	325	1 hour

Cookies:

drop cookies	350	8 to 10 minutes
macaroons	350	8 to 10 minutes
meringues	250	1 hour
refrigerator	350	8 to 10 minutes
rolled	375	8 to 10 minutes
shaped	350	10 to 12 minutes

Pastry:

butter tarts	375	20 minutes
cream puffs	425	20 minutes, then
	350	15 to 20 minutes
double-crust pie	450	10 minutes, then
	350	30 to 40 minutes
eclairs	425	30 minutes, then
	325	15 to 20 minutes
pie & tart shells	450	10 to 15 minutes
turnovers	450	10 minutes, then
	375	30 minutes
meringue (on cooked filling)	350	12 minutes

Table of Imperial Weights and Measures

dash or pinch = less than ⅛ tsp.
¼ tsp. = 1 saltspoon
1 tsp. = 1 coffee spoon
2 tsp. = 1 dessert spoon
3 tsp. = 1 tbsp.
2 tbsp. = ⅛ cup or 1 oz.
4 tbsp. = ¼ cup
5⅓ tbsp. = ⅓ cup
8 tbsp. = ½ cup or 1 tea cup
16 tbsp. = 1 cup
1 fluid oz. = 2 tbsp.
1 pint = 2 cups
1 quart = 2 pints
1 quart = 4 cups
1 gallon = 4 quarts
1 lb. = 16 oz.

Approximate Metric Conversions

Imperial Measurements	Approximate Metric Conversion
⅛ tsp.	0.5 mL
¼ tsp.	1 mL
½ tsp.	2 mL
1 tsp.	5 mL
1 tbsp.	15 mL
1 coffee measure	25 mL
2 tbsp. (1 oz.)	30 mL
¼ cup	50 mL
⅓ cup	80 mL
½ cup	125 mL
⅔ cup	160 mL
¾ cup	180 mL
1 cup	250 mL
1 pint	625 mL

THE POTATO COOKBOOK

1 quart	1000 mL or 1.25 litre
¼ lb.	125 g
½ lb.	250 g
¾ lb.	350 g
1 lb.	500 g

Converting to Metric

To change	**to**	**Multiply by**
teaspoons	mL	5
tablespoons	mL	15
ounces	mL	28
cups	litres	0.24

Casserole sizes

1-quart casserole equals a 1.5-litre casserole
1½-quart casserole equals a 2-litre casserole

Cake pans:

8" square	2 litre
9" square	2.5 litre
12x8x2"	3 litre
13x9x2"	3.5 litre
8" round	1.2 litre
9" round	1.5 litre
jelly roll pan (15x10")	2 litre

Pie pans:

8"	750 mL
9"	1 litre

Tube pans:

8x3"	2 litre
9x4"	3 litre

Loaf pans:
8x4x3"   1.5 litre
9x5x3"   2 litre

Approximate Equivalent Weights

Apples	1 lb.	3 cups sliced or 3 medium-sized
Beans	1 cup (dry)	2½ cups cooked
Bananas	1 lb.	1 cup mashed or 3 medium
Bread	1 lb.	4 cups
Breadcrumbs	1 slice	⅔ cup
Butter:	1 square	½ cup
	1 lb.	2 cups
Cheese, grated	1 lb.	4 cups
Cherries, glaced (halves)	8 oz.	1 cup
Chocolate	1 oz.	1 square
Cocoa	1 lb.	5 cups
Coconut	1 lb.	6 cups
Cornmeal	1 lb.	3 cups
Cornstarch	1 lb.	3½ cups
Crackers:	1 cup	12 graham wafers
	1 cup	18 soda crackers
Cream (whipping)	1 cup	2 cups (whipped)
Currants	1 cup	3 cups
Dates (pitted, chopped)	1 lb.	2½ cups
Flour: all-purpose (sifted)	1 lb.	4 cups
graham	1 lb.	4⅓ cups
rye	1 lb.	4¼ cups
whole wheat	1 lb.	4¼ cups
self-rising	1 lb.	4 cups
Gelatin	¼ oz.	1 envelope or 1 tbsp.
Lard	1 lb.	2⅓ cups
Lemon	1	2 tbsp. grated rind 3 tbsp. juice
Macaroni, spaghetti	1 cup dry	2 cups cooked

           THE POTATO COOKBOOK

Marshmallows	½ lb.	32 large marshmallows or 5 cups miniature
Noodles	1 lb.	7½ cups

(*Noodles do not increase any amount in size when cooked)

Nuts, shelled:		
almonds	1 lb.	3 cups
peanuts	1 lb.	3½ cups
pecan halves	1 lb.	4 cups
walnut halves	1 lb.	4¼ cups
Onion	1 medium	½ cup, chopped
Orange	1 medium	⅓ cup juice
		2¼ tbsp. grated rind
Potatoes	1 lb.	2 large potatoes
		3 medium potatoes
		4 small potatoes
		2¼ cups peeled, diced
		2½ cups peeled, sliced
		2 cups mashed
	2 medium	1 cup mashed
		1½ cups diced
		1¾ cups thinly sliced
	1 medium	⅓ lb. (5 to 6 oz.)
Raisins: seeded	1 lb.	3 cups
seedless	1 lb.	2½ cups
Rhubarb	1 lb.	2 cups chopped
Rice	1 cup, raw	3 cups, cooked
	1 lb.	2 ¼ cups
Rolled oats	1 lb.	6 cups
Shortening	1 lb.	2½ cups
Strawberries	1 quart	3½ cups
Suet	½ lb.	1½ cups chopped
Sugar: brown	1 lb.	2½ cups lightly packed
granulated (white)	1 lb.	2¼ cups
icing sugar	1 lb.	4 cups sifted
Tomatoes	1 lb.	3 medium
		4 small

Common Cooking Terms

á la king = served in a rich cream sauce containing mushrooms and paprika

au gratin = baked or broiled with a bread crumb and/or cheese topping

bake = to cook by dry heat in an oven or oven type appliance

barbecue = to roast meat on a rack or spit, basting with a seasoned sauce

baste = pouring liquid or melted fat over food to prevent drying and to add flavor

batter = mixture of liquid, flour, and other ingredients in thickness ranging from pouring to spreading

beat = to incorporate air into a smooth mixture using a brisk over and over motion with a spoon or electric mixer

blanch = to loosen skins on fruits and nuts by covering in boiling water, then immersing in cold water

blend = to thoroughly combine 2 or more ingredients

boil = to heat a liquid until bubbles continually break on the surface

braise = to cook slowly in a small amount of liquid in a covered dish

bread = to coat with fine bread or cracker crumbs before baking or frying

broil = to cook meat by searing the surface on a broiler or over hot coals

caramelize = to melt sugar slowly over low heat until it becomes a golden brown syrup

chop = to cut food in small pieces with a knife

clarify = to make a liquid clear by skimming and filtering out impurities

coat = to cover food evenly with flour, crumbs, or batter

coddle = to cook food slowly in water heated to just below the boiling point

compote = fruit cooked in syrup and served as a dessert

cool = let food stand at room temperature until no longer warm to the touch

cream = to soften fat, such as butter, with a spoon or mixer, until light and fluffy

cube = to cut a solid food into cubes about ½" or more in size

cut in = to combine solid fat with dry ingredients using 2 knives or a pastry blender

dice = to cut into small cubes of ⅛" to ¼" with a sharp knife on a cutting board

dough = a mixture of flour, liquid, and other ingredients thick enough to knead, pat, or roll out

drain = to remove liquid from a food by placing it in a colander or using a lid

dredge = to coat food with a fine dry substance such as flour

dust	= to sprinkle lightly with sugar or flour
fillet	= a piece of meat, fish, or poultry without bone
flake	= to break into small pieces, usually with a fork
flour	= to coat with flour
flute	= to make a decorative edging around a pie before baking
fold in	= to combine ingredients without releasing air bubbles; using a spoon, go down through the mixture on the far side of the bowl, bring the spoon across the bottom of the bowl and up the near side. Give the bowl a quarter turn with each motion.
fricassée	= food that is browned then simmered or baked in a sauce with vegetables
fry	= to cook in hot fat
	Pan fry = cook in a small amount of fat in a frying pan
	Deep fry = cook in fat deep enough to cover the food
garnish	= to decorate with colorful contrasting food
glacé	= food coated with a sugar syrup.
glaze	= to add luster to a food by coating with a smooth mixture
grate	= to shred food by rubbing it against a grater
grill	= to broil or cook on a rack over hot coals
grind	= to cut or crush in a grinder, blender, or food processor
julienne	= to cut in matchlike strips
knead	= to work dough by pressing with the heel of the hand, folding and stretching. Rotate the dough one-quarter of a turn with each press.
marinade	= a mixture of liquid and seasonings used to tenderize food
melt	= to slowly heat a solid substance until it liquefies
mince	= to grind, chop, or cut into very fine pieces
mix	= to combine ingredients until evenly distributed
pan-broil	= to cook uncovered in a frying pan, draining off fat as it accumulates
parboil	= to partly cook in boiling liquid, then complete the cooking by an other method
pare	= to peel off outer skin
peel	= to strip off or pull away outer covering of fruit or vegetables
poach	= to cook slowly in simmering liquid
pot roast	= a method of cooking cheaper, less tender cuts of meat by browning the surface in fat and then cooking slowly in a small amount of liquid, on top of the stove or in an oven
purée	= to press cooked food through a fine sieve or to mix in a blender
reduce	= to simmer a liquid, uncovered, until some of it evaporates

roast	= to cook meat, uncovered, by dry heat in an oven
sauté	= to brown or cook in small amount of fat
scald	= to heat milk until bubbles form around the edge of the dish or to dip food briefly in boiling water
scallop	= to bake small pieces of food, usually with a cream sauce, in a casserole
score	= to make criss-cross cuts over the surface of a food with a knife
sear	= to cook meat at a very high temperature for a short time, to quickly form a crust on the outer surface
shred	= to cut in long thin strips with a knife or shredder
simmer	= to cook in liquid, just below the boiling point
sliver	= to cut into long thin pieces with a knife
steam	= to cook covered over a small amount of boiling water, so that steam circulates freely around the food
steep	= to let food soak in liquid until liquid absorbs the food's flavor
stew	= to cook covered in boiling water
stir	= to mix together with a spoon using a circular motion
stir fry	= to fry, stirring constantly
toast	= to brown with dry heat in an oven or toaster
whip	= to beat rapidly with a whisk, beater, or mixer to incorporate air; this lightens and increases volume

THE POTATO COOKBOOK

Acknowledgments

Special thanks go to Dr. O. T. Page, Director of Research (1972-1985), International Potato Centre, Lima, Peru; Dr. Samuel Asiedu, Plant Industry Services, P.E.I. Department of Agriculture; Tom and Meredith Hughes, Potato Museum, Washington, D.C.; Irish Potato Marketing Company, Dublin, Ireland; The Potato Board, Denver, Colorado; the P.E.I. Departments of Agriculture and Fisheries, Charlottetown; the P.E.I. Egg Commodity Marketing Board, Charlottetown; the P.E.I. Potato Marketing Board, Charlottetown; Agriculture Canada, Ottawa; Centro Internacional de La Papa (International Potato Centre or CIP), Lima, Peru; Las Damas Del CIP (CIP Women's Club), Lima, Peru; Margaret Weeks and Gloria Wood, home economists with the P.E.I. Department of Agriculture; Harry Fraser, *Fraser's Newsletter;* La Société Saint-Thomas D'Aquin, Summerside, P.E.I.; John Sylvester and Brenda Whiteway, Charlottetown; Ann Thurlow, Charlottetown, for giving the book its title; Cathy Matthews, Valerie Stewart, Lee Fleming, Mary Lou Brinklow, Susan Wright, and Lynn Henry for all their help with proofreading, paste-up, and indexing; my Canadian publisher Libby Oughton and editor Laurie Brinklow, Ragweed Press, Charlottetown; Linkletter Farms Limited, who supplied the potatoes for recipe-testing—not to mention their boundless enthusiasm; Brenda Rogers, without whose help I could not have completed this mammoth undertaking; my husband Allison and son Mark who ate potatoes three meals a day for several weeks without complaint (and never gained an ounce); and all those who contributed anecdotes and recipes as well as much-needed encouragement and support.

Index